Lovely Knits *for* Little Girls

20 Just-Right Patterns, Just For Girls

The Taunton Press, Inc., 63 South Main Street,
PO Box 5506, Newtown, CT 06470-5506
email: tp@taunton.com

Cover Design: Alison Wilkes

First published in the United Kingdom in 2012 by
Collins & Brown
10 Southcombe Street
London W14 0RA

An imprint of Anova Books Company Ltd

Library of Congress Cataloging-in-Publication Data

Sondergaard, Vibe.
  Lovely knits for little girls : 20 just-right patterns, just
for girls / Vibe Sondergaard.
      p. cm.
    ISBN 978-1-60085-503-0 (hardback)
  1. Knitting—Patterns. 2. Knitwear. 3. Girls' clothing.
I. Title.
  TT825.S68 2012
  746.43'2—dc23

                                         2011039817

10 9 8 7 6 5 4 3 2 1

Reproduction by Mission Productions, Hong Kong
Printed and bound by Everbest Printing, China

This book can be ordered direct from
the publisher at www.taunton.com

Lovely Knits *for* Little Girls

20 Just-Right Patterns, Just For Girls

Vibe Ulrik Sondergaard

The Taunton Press

Contents

Introduction

Life can sometimes be a funny mix of chance and coincidence. Although I was taught to knit by my grandma when I was little, it wasn't until my final year of university that I really took it up again. After that my road to a love of knitting was made up of just little things that happened along the way and that slowly formed my direction, and today I feel lucky to have had the support I needed to make my devotion to knitting into a way of living.

Initially it was my desire to combine knitting, children's wear, and photography that sparked the idea for this book. But ultimately it has been the designing and making of the garments, working with beautiful yarns, that I have enjoyed the most.

I tend to get inspired by pretty much everything, so the collection for this book is more an accumulation of ideas of shape, texture, and color, than it is a collection with a set direction. Although some designs are suited to a more experienced knitter, I have included some simpler pieces in the hope that they will spark the less experienced knitter to get those needles glowing—sometimes a new technique is easier than you think.

I wish you all the best in knitting lovely knits for your own little girls.

Vibe U. Søndergaard

Sweaters

Clara Alpaca and Cotton Butterfly Sweater

A simple stockinette stitch sweater with flared sleeves to add a pretty touch. Perfect if you want something that's easy to knit with just a bit of shaping.

MEASUREMENTS

Size	3–4 yrs	5–6 yrs	7–8 yrs
To fit chest	23 in	23¾ in	25¼ in
Finished chest measurement	25½ in	26¼ in	29½ in

YARN

2(3:3) x 1¾ oz balls of Rowan Alpaca Cotton in Smoked Salmon 407

MATERIALS

Pair of US size 6 knitting needles
Spare US size 6 knitting needle
3 stitch holders
Tapestry needle

GAUGE

16 sts and 24 rows to 4 in over st st using US size 6 needles

ABBREVIATIONS

See page 140

BACK

Cast on 52(54:60) sts.
Row 1: [K1, p1] to end of row.
Rep row 1, 3 times more.
Row 5: Knit.
Row 6: Purl.
These last two rows establish st st.
Cont in st st until back measures 7½(9½:11) in, ending with a WS row.
Shape armholes
Bind off 3 sts at beg of next 2 rows. *46(48:54) sts*
Dec 1 st at each end of next 2 rows. *42(44:50) sts*
Cont in st st until work measures 2½(2¾:3) in from start of armhole, ending with a WS row.
Shape neck
Next row: K9(9:12), k2tog, k1, turn (leave rem 30(32:35) sts on a spare needle).
Next row: P1, p2tog, p to end of row. *10(10:13) sts*
Shape shoulders
Next row: Bind off 3 sts, k to end of row. *7(7:10) sts*
Next row: Purl.
Next row: Slip 1 st from left-hand needle to right-hand needle and bind off all sts.
RS facing, slip 18(20:20) sts onto stitch holder and re-join yarn to rem sts on spare needle.
Next row: K1, ssk, k to end of row. *11(11:14) sts*
Next row: P8(8:11), p2tog, p1. *10(10:13) sts*
Next row: Knit.

Next row: Bind off 3 sts, p to end of row. *7(7:10) sts*
Next row: K7(7:10), turn, slip 1 st from left-hand needle to right-hand needle and bind off all sts.

FRONT

Cast on 52(54:60) sts.
Row 1: [K1, p1] to end of row.
Rep row 1, 3 times more.
Row 5: Knit.
Row 6: Purl.
These last two rows establish st st.
Cont in st st until front measures 7½(9½:11) in, ending with a WS row.
Shape armholes
Bind off 3 sts at beg of next 2 rows. *46(48:54) sts*
Dec 1 st at each end of next 2 rows. *42(44:50) sts*
Cont in st st until work measures 8 rows less than Back to shape shoulders, ending with a WS row.
Next row: K15(15:18), k2tog, k1, turn (leave rem 24(26:29) sts on a spare needle).
Dec 1 st at neck edge on every row for next 7 rows. *10(10:13) sts*
Shape shoulder
Next row: Bind off 3 sts, k to end of row.
Next row: Purl.
Next row: Slip 1 st from left-hand needle to right-hand needle and bind off all sts.

Clara Alpaca and Cotton Butterfly Sweater

RS facing, slip 6(8:8) sts onto stitch holder and re-join yarn to rem sts on spare needle.
Next row: K1, ssk, k to end of row.
Dec 1 st at neck edge on every row for next 7 rows. *10(10:13) sts*
Next row: Knit.
Next row: Bind off 3 sts, p to end of row.
Next row: Knit.
Next row: Slip 1 st from left-hand needle to right-hand needle and bind off all sts.

SLEEVE (MAKE TWO)

(Sleeves are worked from the top so there is a lot of increasing at the start to shape sleeve head.)
Cast on 6(8:12) sts.
Row 1: Purl.
Row 2: [Inc] twice, k to last 2 sts, [inc] twice.
Row 3: [Inc] twice, p to last 2 sts, [inc] twice.
Rep rows 2–3 once more. *22(24:28) sts*
Row 6: Knit.
Row 7: Inc, p to last st, inc.
Row 8: Inc, k to last st, inc. *26(28:32) sts*
Row 9: Purl.
Row 10: Inc, k to last st, inc.
Row 11: Inc, p to last st, inc. *30(32:36) sts*
Row 12: Knit.
Rep rows 7–12 once more, then rep rows 7–9 once more. *42(44:48) sts*

Row 22: Inc, k to last st, inc. *44(46:50) sts*
Row 23: Purl.
Rep rows 22–23 twice more. *48(50:54) sts*
Row 28: K1, ssk, k18(19:21), k2tog, k1, turn (leave rem 24(25:27) sts on a stitch holder). *22(23:25) sts on needle*
Row 29: P to last 2 sts, p2tog.
Row 30: K1, ssk, k to last 2 sts, k2tog.
Row 31: P to last 2 sts, p2tog.
Row 32: K1, ssk, k to last 2 sts, k2tog.
Cont to dec as set until 4 sts rem.
Row 41(42:43): [Work 2tog] twice.
Row 42(43:44): Work 2tog and fasten off.
RS facing, slip 24(25:27) sts from stitch holder onto needle and re-join yarn.
Row 28: K1, ssk, k18(19:21), k2tog, k1. *22(23:25) sts*
Row 29: P2tog, p to end of row.
Row 30: K1, ssk, k to last 2 sts, k2tog.
Complete to match first side.

Weave in loose ends.
Steam the pieces following directions on the yarn label.
Sew up one shoulder seam.

Neckband
Starting at the open shoulder seam with RS facing, pick up 76(80:84) sts, including the stitches left on the stitch holders, around the neck.
Row 1: [K1, p1] to end of row.
Rep row 1 twice more.
Bind off.

Sew up the other shoulder seam.

Sew up the split in the middle of each sleeve. Pin the cast on edge of each sleeve into the armhole above bound off sts at underarm, easing it in so that it is slightly puffed. Sew the sleeves in place. Sew up side seams to lower edge of body.

Clara Alpaca and Cotton Butterfly Sweater

Ruth Aran and Bobble Sweater

This is a classic sweater with a modern twist in the shape of the puffed sleeves. Knitting it up in a bright color would make it even more individual.

MEASUREMENTS

Size	3–4 yrs	5–6 yrs	7–8 yrs
To fit chest	22½ in	24 in	25¼ in
Finished chest measurement	23 in	25½ in	28¼ in
Finished sleeve seam	2½ in	2½ in	2½ in

YARN

4(5:5) x 1¾ oz balls of UK Alpaca DK in Fawn 03

MATERIALS

Pair each of US size 3 and US size 6 knitting needles
Cable needle
Stitch holder
Tapestry needle

GAUGE

30 sts and 32 rows to 4 in over cable patt using US size 6 needles

ABBREVIATIONS

C4B–slip next 2 sts onto cable needle and hold at back of work, knit next 2 sts from left-hand needle, then knit 2 sts from cable needle.
C4F–slip next 2 sts onto cable needle and hold in front of work, knit next 2 sts from left-hand needle, then knit 2 sts from cable needle.
C6B–slip next 3 sts onto cable needle and hold at back of work, knit next 3 sts from left-hand needle, then knit 3 sts from cable needle.
C6F–slip next 3 sts onto cable needle and hold in front of work, knit next 3 sts from left-hand needle, then knit 3 sts from cable needle.
See also page 140

BACK

Using US size 3 needles, cast on 88(97:109) sts.
Row 1: Knit.
Row 2: [K1, p2] to last st, k1.
Row 3: [P1, k2] to last st, p1.
Row 4: As row 2.
Row 5: As row 3, but inc 1 st on size 5–6 and dec 1 st on size 7–8.
88(98:108) sts
Change to US size 6 needles.
Row 6 (RS): P2(7:8), [k12, p1(1:2), k4, p1(1:2)] 4 times, k12, p2(7:8).

Row 7: K2(7:8), [p12, k1(1:2), p4, k1(1:2)] 4 times, p12, k2(7:8).
Row 8: P2(7:8), C6B, C6F, p1(1:2), C4B, p1(1:2), C6B, C6F, p1(1:2), C4F, p1(1:2), C6B, C6F, p1(1:2), C4B, p1(1:2), C6B, C6F, p1(1:2), C4F, p1(1:2), C6B, C6F, p2(7:8).
Row 9: As row 7.
Rep rows 6–9 until work measures 10(10¼:11) in from cast on edge, ending with a WS row.
Shape armholes
Keeping patt correct as set, shape as folls:
Bind off 2 sts at beg of next 2 rows. *84(94:104) sts*
Dec 1 st at each end of next 2 rows. *80(90:100) sts*
Work in patt until work measures 14½(15¼:16½) in from cast on edge.
Shape shoulders
RS facing, bind off 15 sts, patt to end of row.
Bind off 15 sts, patt to end of row. *50(60:70) sts*
Bind off.

FRONT

Using US size 3 needles, cast on 75(81:90) sts.
Row 1: Knit.
Row 2: [K1, p2] to end of row.
Row 3: [K2, p1] to end of row.
Row 4: As row 2.
Row 5: As row 3, but inc 1 st on sizes 3–4 and 5–6. *76(82:90) sts*

Ruth Aran and Bobble Sweater

Change to US size 6 needles.

Row 6 (RS): P2(5:6), k8, p1(1:2), k4, p1(1:2), k8, p1(1:2), k4, p18, k4, p1(1:2), k8, p1(1:2), k4, p1(1:2), k8, p2(5:6).

Row 7: K2(5:6), p8, k1(1:2), p4, k1(1:2), p8, k1(1:2), p4, k1, [(k1, p1, k1) all into next st, p3tog] 4 times, k1, p4, k1(1:2), p8, k1(1:2), p4, k1(1:2), p8, k2(5:6).

Row 8: P2(5:6), C4B, C4F, p1(1:2), C4B, p1(1:2), C4B, C4F, p1(1:2), C4F, p18, C4B, p1(1:2), C4B, C4F, p1(1:2), C4F, p1(1:2), C4B, C4F, p2(5:6).

Row 9: K2(5:6), p8, k1(1:2), p4, k1(1:2), p8, k1(1:2), p4, k1, [p3tog, (k1, p1, k1) all into next st] 4 times, k1, p4, k1(1:2), p8, k1(1:2), p4, k1(1:2), p8, k2(5:6).

Rep rows 6–9 until work measures 10(10¼:11) in from cast on edge, ending with a WS row.

Shape armholes

Keeping patt correct as set, shape as folls:

Bind off 2 sts at beg of next 2 rows. *72(78:86) sts*

Dec 1 st at each end of next 2 rows. *68(74:82) sts*

Work in patt until work measures 12¾(13½:15) in from cast on edge.

Shape neck

Keeping patt correct as set, work 23 sts, turn (leave rem 45(51:59) sts on a stitch holder).

Dec 1 st at neck edge on next 8 rows. *15 sts*

Patt 3 rows.

Bind off.

Slip rem 45(51:59) sts from stitch holder onto needle and re-join yarn.

Bind off 22(28:36) sts, patt to end of row. *23 sts*

Dec 1 st at neck edge on next 8 rows. *15 sts*

Patt 4 rows.

Bind off.

SLEEVE (MAKE TWO)

Using US size 3 needles, cast on 54(60:63) sts.
Row 1: Knit.
Row 2: [K1, p2] to end of row.
Row 3: [K2, p1] to end of row.
Row 4: As row 2.
Row 5: As row 3, but inc 1 st on size 7–8.
54(60:64) sts
Change to US size 6 needles.
Row 6 (RS): K13(16:18), p1, k6, p1, k12, p1, k6,
p1, k13(16:18).
Row 7: P13(16:18), k1, p6, k1, p12, k1, p6, k1,
p13(16:18).
Row 8: K13(16:18), p1, C6B, p1, C6B, C6F, p1,
C6F, p1, k13(16:18).
Row 9: As row 7.
Rep rows 6–9 twice more, then rep rows 6–7 once
more, **at the same time** inc and work into st st 1 st
at each end of every alt row. *64(70:74) sts*
Shape sleeve head
Keeping patt correct as set, shape as folls:
Bind off 2 sts at beg of next 2 rows. *60(66:70) sts*
Dec 1 st at each end of next and every alt row for
20 rows. *40(46:50) sts*
Cont in st st.
Dec 1 st at each end of every row for 10 rows.
20(26:30) sts
Bind off.

FINISHING

Weave in loose ends.
Steam the pieces following directions on the
yarn label.
Sew up one shoulder seam.

Neckband
Using US size 3 needles and with RS facing, pick
up and knit 81(96:111) sts around the neck.
Row 1: [K2, p1] to end of row.
Row 2: [K1, p2] to end of row.
Rep rows 1–2 twice more, then row 1 once more.
Bind off.

Sew up the other shoulder seam.

Pin each sleeve into an armhole, easing it in so
that it is slightly puffed at the top. Sew the sleeves
in place.
Sew up the underarm and side seams from end of
sleeve to lower edge of body.

Ruth Aran and Bobble Sweater

Carolina High-neck Sweater with Ribbon

On chilly days it's lovely to have a sweater that covers the neck without being too clingy—especially when it's made in a gorgeous, soft yarn.

MEASUREMENTS

Size	3–4 yrs	5–6 yrs	7–8 yrs
To fit chest	23 in	24 in	25¼ in
Finished chest measurement	24¾ in	26 in	27 in
Finished sleeve seam	8¾ in	10 in	10¼ in

YARN

6(7:7) x 1¾ oz balls of Rowan Lima in Peru 889

MATERIALS

Pair each of US size 6 and US size 8 knitting needles
2 long stitch holders
Tapestry needle
Approx 52 in of 1 in ribbon for the tie
Safety pin or bodkin

GAUGE

23 sts and 24 rows to 4 in over patt using US size 8 needles

MK—make knot: p3tog leaving sts on needle, yo, then purl the same sts together again.
See also page 140

DAISY STITCH PATTERN

(Worked over multiple of 4 sts)
Row 1 (RS): Knit.
Row 2: [K1, MK] to end of row.
Row 3: Knit.
Row 4: K1, p1, [k1, MK] to last 2 sts, k1, p1.

BACK

**Using US size 6 needles, cast on 72(76:80) sts.
Row 1: Knit.
Rows 2–3: [K1, p1] to end of row.
Change to US size 8 needles.
Work in daisy stitch patt until work measures
9½(10¼:11) in from cast on edge.
Shape armholes
Keeping patt correct as set, shape as folls:
Bind off 2 sts at beg of next 2 rows. *68(72:76) sts*
Dec 1 st at each end of next 2 rows. *64(68:72) sts*
Work in patt until work measures 4(4½:4¾) in
from start of armhole shaping.

Carolina High-neck Sweater with Ribbon

Shape shoulders

Dec 1 st at each end of every row for 8 rows.**

48(52:56) sts

Change to US size 6 needles.

Next row: [K1, p1] to end of row.

Rep last row 16 times more.

Bind off.

FRONT

Work as for Back from ** to **. *48(52:56) sts*

Change to US size 6 needles.

Next row: [K1, p1] 12(13:14) times, turn (leave rem sts on a stitch holder).

Next row: [K1, p1] to end of row.

Rep last row 5 times more.

Cut yarn and leave these sts on a stitch holder.

Slip sts on first stitch holder onto a needle and re-join yarn.

Next row: [K1, p1] to end of row.

Rep last row 7 times more, then work across sts from second stitch holder. *48(52:56) sts*

Next row: [K1, p1] to end of row.

Rep last row 8 times more.

Bind off.

SLEEVE (MAKE TWO)

Using US size 6 needles, cast on 44(52:52) sts.
Row 1: Knit.
Rows 2–3: [K1, p1] to end of row.
Change to US size 8 needles.
Work in daisy stitch patt and **at the same time**
inc and work into patt 1 st at each end of every
10th row until there are 46(54:56) sts, then work
even until work measures 8¾(10:10¼) in from
cast on edge.
Bind off 2 sts at beg of next 2 rows. *42(50:52) sts*
Dec 1 st at each end of every row for next
12 rows. *18(26:28) sts*
Bind off. (When casting off, *bind off 2 sts, then
work a k2tog and do the usual passing over, rep
from * across the row to create a more even line.)

FINISHING

Weave in loose ends.
Steam the pieces following directions on the
yarn label.
Sew up the shoulder seams and neck rib. Fold the
neck rib in half to the WS and slip stitch bound
off edge in place to make a channel for the ribbon.
Sew the sleeves into the armholes. Sew up the
underarm and side seams from end of sleeve to
lower edge of body.
Using a safety pin or a bodkin, slip the ribbon
through the channel and tie a bow in the front.

Carolina High-neck Sweater with Ribbon

Nora Wide Aran Sweater with Ribbon

The contemporary color and shape of this sweater combine beautifully with the traditional Aran pattern. You can work the rib to go all around the neck if you wish; I just thought adding the ribbon makes for a pretty detail.

MEASUREMENTS

Size	3–4 yrs	5–6 yrs	7–8 yrs
To fit chest	23 in	24 in	25¼ in
Finished chest measurement	23¾ in	25 in	27½ in
Finished sleeve seam	6¾ in	7½ in	10 in

YARN

7(7:8) x 1¾ oz balls of Debbie Bliss Eco Aran in Lemon 32619

MATERIALS

Pair each of US size 3 and US size 6 knitting needles
Cable needle
Short US size 3 circular needle
Tapestry needle
Approx 28 in of 1 in ribbon for the tie
Sewing needle and thread

GAUGE

22 sts and 24 rows to 4 in over patt using US size 6 needles

C4B—slip next 2 sts onto cable needle and hold at
back of work, knit next 2 sts from left-hand
needle, then knit 2 sts from cable needle.
C4F—slip next 2 sts onto cable needle and hold in
front of work, knit next 2 sts from left-hand
needle, then knit 2 sts from cable needle.
See also page 140

CABLE PATTERN

(Worked over multiple of 8 sts)
Row 1: Knit.
Row 2: Purl.
Row 3: [C4B, C4F] to end of row.
Row 4: Purl.
Row 5: Knit.
Row 6: Purl.
Row 7: [C4F, C4B] to end of row.
Row 8: Purl.

BACK AND FRONT (BOTH ALIKE)

Using US size 3 needles, cast on 82(90:98) sts.
Row 1: Knit.
Row 2: [K1, p1] to end of row.
Rep row 2, 5 times more.

Change to US size 6 needles.

Row 7: Knit.

Row 8: P1, p2tog, p to last 3 sts, p2tog, p1.

Starting with row 3 of cable patt (C4B, C4F), work in patt, **at the same time** dec 1 st at each end of every 5th row until there are 64(70:78) sts, working in st st when there are insufficient sts to work a whole cable.

Shape raglan armholes

Row 55(63:63): Bind off 3 sts, patt to end of row. *61(67:75) sts*

Row 56(64:64): Bind off 3 sts, patt to end of row. *58(64:72) sts*

Rows 57–58(65–66:65–66): Work in patt.

Rows 59–78(67–86:67–86): Keeping patt correct as set, dec 1 st at each end of next and every alt row for 20 rows. *38(44:52) sts*

Bind off.

Sleeve (make two)

Using US size 3 needles, cast on 42 sts.

Row 1: Knit.

Row 2: [K1, p1] to end of row.

Rep row 2, 5 times more.

Change to US size 6 needles.

Row 7: Knit.

Row 8: Purl.

Row 9: K1, [C4B, C4F] 5 times, k1.

Nora Wide Aran Sweater with Ribbon

Row 10: Purl.
Row 11: Knit.
Row 12: Purl.
Row 13: Inc, (C4F, C4B) 5 times, inc. *44 sts*
Row 14: Purl.
Keeping cable patt correct as set, inc and work into patt 1 st at each end of every 6th row until there are 52(54:58) sts.
Work 5(3:5) rows even.

Shape raglan sleeve top
Row 43(47:61): Bind off 3 sts, patt to end of row. *49(51:55) sts*
Row 44(48:62): Bind off 3 sts, patt to end of row. *46(48:52) sts*
Rows 45–46(49–50:63–64): Work in patt.
Rows 47–66(51–70:65–84): Keeping patt correct as set, dec 1 st at each end of every alt row for 20 rows. *26(28:30) sts*
Bind off.

FINISHING

Weave in loose ends.
Steam the pieces following directions on the yarn label.
Sew up the raglan seams to join the back, front and both sleeves.

Neckband
Mark the center back neck. Using US size 3 circular needle, with RS facing and starting ¾ in to one side of marked center back neck, pick up 56(60:62) sts around the neck, finishing ¾ in before returning to center back neck (so a 1½ in gap straddles center back neck).
Row 1: [K1, p1] to end of row.
Rep row 1, 6 times more.
Bind off.

Sew up the underarm and side seams from end of sleeve to lower edge of body.
Sew a length of ribbon to each side of the rib at the back neck and tie.

Nora Wide Aran Sweater with Ribbon

Matilda Round-neck Textured Sweater

This piece is a bit advanced, but once you get into the pattern, it is very repetitive and not difficult to follow; indeed, it can almost be meditative. If you like to knit texture, this is one to try out.

MEASUREMENTS

Size	3–4 yrs	5–6 yrs	7–8 yrs
To fit chest	23 in	24 in	25¼ in
Finished chest measurement	24 in	26 in	28¼ in
Finished sleeve seam	9 in	10 in	12 in

YARN

6(6:7) x 1¾ oz balls of Rowan Cashsoft DK in Weather 425

MATERIALS

Pair each of US size 6 and US size 10 knitting needles
2(1:2) cable needles
Tapestry needle

GAUGE

26 sts and 28 rows to 4 in over central cable patt using US size 6 needles

C3B–slip next 2 sts onto cable needle and hold at back of work, knit next 1 st from left-hand needle, then knit 2 sts from cable needle.

C3F–slip next 1 st onto cable needle and hold in front of work, knit next 2 sts from left-hand needle, then knit 1 st from cable needle.

MK–make knot: p3tog leaving sts on needle, yo, then purl the same sts together again.

See also page 140

FRONT AND BACK (BOTH ALIKE)

With US size 6 needles, cast on 68(76:84) sts.
Row 1: Purl.
Row 1: Knit.
Rows 3–5: Rep rows 1–2, then rep row 1 again.
Row 6: K21, [p2, C3F, C3B] 3(4:5) times, p2, k21.
Row 7: [K1, MK] 5 times, k1, [k2, p6] 3(4:5) times, k2, [k1, MK] 5 times, k1.
Row 8: As row 6.
Row 9: K1, p1, [k1, MK] 4 times, k1, p1, k3, [p6, k2] 3(4:5) times, k1, p1, [k1, MK] 4 times, k1, p1, k1.
Rows 6–9 form central cable panel with daisy stitch at side edges.
Rep rows 6–9 until work measures 8¾(9½:11) in from cast on edge, ending with a row 9.

Size 3–4 only
Next row: K21, [p2, slip 1 st onto cable needle and hold in front of work, knit next 2 sts from left-hand needle, slip next 2 sts onto another cable needle and hold at back of work, then knit 1 st from first cable needle tog with next st from left-hand needle, then knit 2 sts from rem cable needle] 3 times, k21. *65 sts*
Size 5–6 only
Next row: K21, [p2, C3F, C3B] twice, inc 1 st purlwise, p1, [C3F, C3B, p2] twice, k21. *77 sts*
Size 7–8 only
Next row: K21, p2, C3F, C3B, p2, [slip 1 st onto cable needle and hold in front of work, knit next 2 sts from left-hand needle, slip next 2 sts onto another cable needle and hold at back of work, then knit 1 st from first cable needle tog with next st from left-hand needle, then knit 2 sts from rem cable needle, p2] 3 times, C3F, C3B, p2, k21. *81 sts*
All sizes
Next row: [K1, MK] to last st, k1.
Shape raglan armholes
Next row (RS): Keeping daisy patt correct as set across all sts, bind off 3 sts, patt to end of row. *62(74:79) sts*
Next row: Bind off 3 sts, patt to end of row. *59(71:75) sts*
Dec 1 st at each end of next and every alt (RS) row for next 12 rows. *47(59:63) sts*
Bind off.

Matilda Round-neck Textured Sweater

Sleeve (make two)

Using US size 6 needles, cast on 52 sts.

Row 1: Purl.

Row 2 (RS): K9, p2, [C3F, C3B, p2] 4 times, k9.

Row 3: [K1, MK] twice, k3, (p6, k2) 4 times, [k1, MK] twice, k1.

Row 4: K9, p2, [C3F, C3B, p2] 4 times, k9.

Row 5: K1, p1, k1, MK, k1, p1, k3, [p6, k2] 4 times, k1, p1, k1, MK, k1, p1, k1.

Rows 2–5 form central cable panel with daisy stitch at side edges.

Inc and work into daisy patt 1 st at each end of next and every foll 10th row until there are 62(64:68) sts. Cont without shaping until work measures 9(10:12) in from cast on edge, ending with a WS row.

Shape raglan sleeve top

Next row (RS): Bind off 3 sts, patt 28(29:31) including st used to bind off, inc in next st, patt to end of row. *60(62:66) sts*

Next row: Bind off 3 sts, patt to end of row. *57(59:63) sts*

Working across all sts in daisy patt as set, dec 1 st at each end of next and every alt (RS) row for next 12 rows. *45(47:51) sts*

Bind off.

Neckband

Sew up the pieces along the raglan seams.
Using US size 10 needles and 2 strands of yarn,
cast on 14 sts.
Row 1: Purl.
Row 2 (RS): C3F, C3B, p2, C3F, C3B.
Row 3: P6, k2, p6.
Row 4: C3F, C3B, p2, C3F, C3B.
Row 5: P6, k2, turn.
Row 6: P2, C3F, C3B (when working the first
purl stitch, purl it together with a loop from the
previous row so as not to leave a gap between sts).
Row 7: P6, k2, p6.
Rep rows 2–7 until shortest edge fits entire
neck edge.
Bind off on the WS.

Finishing

Weave in loose ends.
Press the pieces following directions on the
yarn label.
Sew the ends of the neckband together. Pin the
neckband to the neck, matching the neckband
seam to the back right raglan seam. Sew the
neckband in place.
Sew up the underarm and side seams from end of
sleeve to lower edge of body.

Matilda Round-neck Textured Sweater

Cardigans

Zoe Fan Stitch Jacket

A little jacket in an easy pattern that creates a lovely texture.

Measurements

Size	3–4 yrs	5–6 yrs	7–8 yrs
To fit chest	23 in	24 in	25¼ in
Knitted measurements	26 in	28¼ in	30¾ in
Finished sleeve seam	9 in	10 in	11 in

Yarn

4(5:5) x 1¾ oz balls of Rowan by Amy Butler Belle Organic DK in Zinc 017

Materials

Pair of US size 6 knitting needles
Long stitch holder
Tapestry needle
Approx 28 in of 1 in ribbon for the tie
Sewing needle and thread
Crochet hook (optional)

Gauge

20 sts and 28 rows to 4 in over patt using US size 6 needles

Abbreviations

See page 140

BODY

Cast on 110(122:134) sts.

Row 1: Knit.

Row 2: Purl.

Row 3: K1, *[yo, k1] twice, k2tog 4 times, [yo, k1] twice, rep from * to last st, k1.

Row 4: K1, yo, k to last st, yo, k1. *112(124:136) sts*

Row 5: Knit.

Row 6: P1, yo, p to last st, yo, p1. *114(126:138) sts*

Row 7: K3, *[yo, k1] twice, k2tog 4 times, [yo, k1] twice, rep from * to last 3 sts, k3.

Row 8: K1, yo, k to last st, yo, k1. *116(128:140) sts*

Row 9: Knit.

Row 10: P1, yo, p to last st, yo, p1. *118(130:142) sts*

Row 11: K5, *[yo, k1] twice, k2tog 4 times, [yo, k1] twice, rep from * to last 5 sts, k5.

Row 12: K1, yo, k to last st, yo, k1. *120(132:144) sts*

Row 13: Knit.

Row 14: P1, yo, p to last st, yo, p1. *122(134:146) sts*

Row 15: K1, *[k2tog] twice, [yo, k1] 4 times, [k2tog] twice, rep from * to last st, k1.

Row 16: K1, yo, k to last st, yo, k1. *124(136:148) sts*

Row 17: Knit.

Row 18: Purl.

Row 19: K2, *[k2tog] twice, [yo, k1] 4 times, [k2tog] twice, rep from * to last 2 sts, k2.

Zoe Fan Stitch Jacket

Row 20: Knit.

Row 21: Knit.

Row 22: P1, yo, p to last st, yo, p1. *126(138:150) sts*

Row 23: K3, *[k2tog] twice, [yo, k1] 4 times, [k2tog] twice, rep from * to last 3 sts, k3.

Row 24: K1, yo, k to last st, yo, k1. *128(140:152) sts*

Row 25: Knit.

Row 26: Purl.

Row 27: K4, *[k2tog] twice, [yo, k1] 4 times, [k2tog] twice, rep from * to last 4 sts, k4.

Row 28: K1, yo, k to last stich, yo, k1. *130(142:152) sts*

Row 29: Knit.

Row 30: P1, yo, p to last st, yo, p1. *132(144:154) sts*

Row 31: *[Yo, k1] twice, [k2tog] 4 times, [yo, k1] twice, rep from * to end of row.

Row 32: Knit.

Row 33: Knit.

Row 34: Purl.

Row 35: Keeping patt correct as set, work until body measures 10¼(11:12¾) in from cast on edge, ending with a WS row.

RIGHT FRONT

Work 40(44:48) sts in patt, turn (leave rem sts on a stitch holder).

Shape armhole

Next row: Bind off 2 sts, patt to end of row. *38(42:46) sts*

Dec 1 st at armhole edge on next 2 rows. *36(40:44) sts*

Patt 14 rows.

Shape neck

**RS facing, bind off 3 sts at beg of next row.

Patt 1 row.**

Rep from ** to ** 6 times more. *15(19:23) sts*

Patt 3 rows.

Bind off.

BACK

Slip 52(56:60) sts from stitch holder onto needle.

Shape armholes

Next row (RS): Bind off 2 sts and work rest of row, keeping patt correct as set. *50(54:58) sts*

Next row: Bind off 2 sts, patt to end of row. *48(52:56) sts*

Dec 1 st at each end of next 2 rows. *44(48:52) sts*

Patt 30 rows.

Next row: Bind off 15(19:23) sts, patt to end of row.

Next row: Bind off 15(19:23) sts, patt to end of row.

Bind off all sts.

LEFT FRONT

Slip rem 40(44:48) sts from holder onto needle.
Shape armhole
Next row: Bind off 2 sts and work rest of row, keeping patt correct as set. *38(42:46) sts*
Dec 1 st at armhole edge on next 2 rows. *36(40:44) sts*
Patt 14 rows.
**WS facing, bind off 3 sts at beg of next row.
Patt 1 row.**
Rep from ** to ** 6 times more. *15(19:23) sts*
Patt 3 rows.
Bind off.

SLEEVE (MAKE TWO)

Cast on 38 sts.
Row 1: Knit.
Row 2: Purl.
Row 3: K1, *[yo, k1] twice, [k2tog] 4 times, [yo, k1] twice, rep from * to last st, k1.
Row 4: Knit.
Keeping patt correct as set, inc 1 st at each end of next and every 10th(10th:12th) row until there are 50 sts.
Cont without shaping until work measures 9(10:11) in from cast on edge, ending with a WS row.

Shape sleeve top
Bind off 2 sts at beg of next 2 rows. *46 sts*
Dec 1 st at each end of next 16 rows. *14 sts*
Bind off all sts.

COLLAR

Cast on 62 sts.
Row 1: Knit.
Row 2: Purl.
Row 3: K1, *[yo, k1] twice, [k2tog] 4 times,
[yo, k1] twice, rep from * to last st, k1.
Row 4: Knit.
Row 5: Knit.
Row 6: Purl.
Rep rows 3–6 twice more, then rep rows 3–5
once more.
Bind off purlwise.

FINISHING

Weave in loose ends.
Press the pieces following directions on the
yarn label.
Sew up the shoulder seams. Pin the sleeves into
the armholes and sew them in place.
Matching the WS of the center back neck to the
WS of the center of the collar, pin and then sew
the collar to the jacket. You can work a row of
crochet around the edges of the jacket and the
cuffs if you wish. To tie front, cut ribbon in half
and sew one length to right front edge just below
armhole and sew other length to left side seam at
same height.

Zoe Fan Stitch Jacket

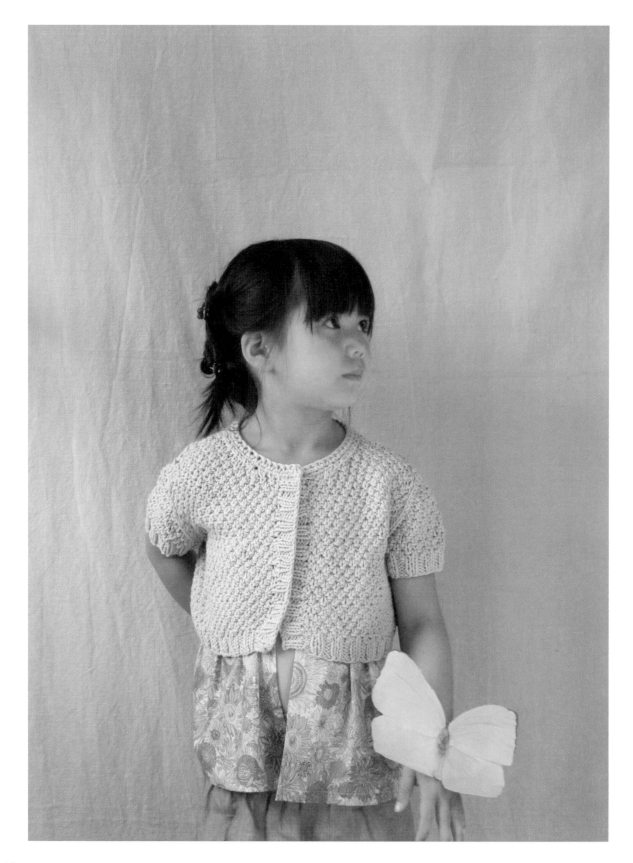

Sophia Elf Cardigan with Fabric

The back of this cardigan is sure to get lots of admiring attention. If you attach the fabric to the knit with buttons, you can easily take it off and wash it, and even change it if you find another fabric you prefer.

MEASUREMENTS

Size	3–4 yrs	5–6 yrs	7–8 yrs
To fit chest	23 in	24 in	25¼ in
Finished chest measurement	24 in	26 in	28¼ in

YARN

3(3:4) x 1¾ oz balls of Debbie Bliss Eco Aran in Pale Sky 32607

MATERIALS

Pair each of US size 3 and US size 6 knitting needles
Cable needle
2 stitch holders
F/5 crochet hook (optional)
Tapestry needle
12(14:16) in of linen or lightweight cotton fabric measuring at least 43 in wide; the one used here is a Liberty fabric called Small Susanna
Bias binding
Sewing thread
Sewing machine (alternatively hand stitch the fabric ruffle)
Sewing needle
Choice of snap, button, hook and eye, or ribbon

GAUGE

16 sts and 22 rows to 4 in over st st using US size 6 needles

C4B–slip next 2 sts onto cable needle and hold at back of work, knit next 2 sts from left-hand needle, then knit 2 sts from cable needle.
C4F–slip next 2 sts onto cable needle and hold in front of work, knit next 2 sts from left-hand needle, then knit 2 sts from cable needle.
See also page 140

Note: The body of the garment is knitted in two pieces that are later joined into one piece to avoid seams.

DOUBLE SEED STITCH PATTERN

(Worked over even number of sts)
Rows 1–2: [K1, p1] to end of row.
Rows 3–4: [P1, k1] to end of row.

LEFT FRONT AND LEFT BACK

Using US size 3 needles, cast on 42(46:50) sts.
Row 1: K8, [p2, k2] to last 2 sts, p2.
Row 2: [K2, p2] to last 10 sts, k2, p8.
Rep rows 1–2 twice more.
Change to US size 6 needles.
Row 7: C4B, C4F, [k1, p1] to end of row.

Row 8: [K1, p1] to last 8 sts, p8.
Row 9: K8, [p1, k1] to end of row.
Row 10: [P1, k1] to last 8 sts, p8.
Rep rows 7–10, 3(3:4) times more.
Row 23(23:27): As row 7.
Row 24(24:28): As row 8.
Row 25(25:29): K8, inc, [k1, p1] to last st, k1. *43(47:51) sts*
Row 26(26:30): [P1, k1] to last 9 sts, p9.
Row 27(27:31): C4B, C4F, inc, [k1, p1] to end of row. *44(48:52) sts*
Row 28(28:32): Keeping double seed patt correct as set, patt to last 8 sts, p8.
Row 29(29:33): K8, inc, patt to end of row. *45(49:53) sts*
Row 30(30:34): Patt to last 8 sts, p8.
Row 31(31:35): As row 27(27:31). *46(50:54) sts*
Row 32(32:36): As row 28(28:29).
Row 33(33:37): As row 29(29:30). *47(51:55) sts*
Left front side
Row 34(34:38): Patt 26(28:30) sts, turn (leave rem 21(23:25) sts on a stitch holder).
Row 35(35:39): Bind off 2 sts, patt to end of row. *24(26:28) sts*
Row 36(36:40): Patt to last 3 sts, p2tog, p1. *23(25:27) sts*
Row 37(37:41): K1, ssk, patt to end of row. *22(24:26) sts*
Rows 38–49(38–49:42–53): Patt to end of row.

Sophia Elf Cardigan with Fabric

Row 50(50:54): Bind off 4 sts (1 st on right-hand needle), p2tog, patt to end of row. *17(19:21) sts*

Row 51(51:55): Patt to last 3 sts, k2tog, k1. *16(18:20) sts*

Row 52(52:56): P1, p2tog, patt to end of row. *15(17:19) sts*

Row 53(53:57): As row 51(51:55). *14(16:18) sts*

Row 54(54:58): As row 52(52:56). *13(15:17) sts*

Row 55(55:59): As row 51(51:55). *12(14:16) sts*

Row 56(56:60): As row 52(52:56). *11(13:15) sts*

Row 57(57:61): As row 51(51:55). *10(12:14) sts*

Row 58(58:62): As row 52(52:56). *9(11:13) sts*

Rows 59–61(59–61:63–65): Patt to end of row.

Row 62(62:66): Patt 6 sts, turn.

Row 63(63:67): Patt to end of row.

Bind off all sts.

RIGHT FRONT AND RIGHT BACK

Using US size 3 needles, cast on 42(46:50) sts.

Row 1: [P2, k2] to last 10 sts, p2, k8.

Row 2: P8, [k2, p2] to last 2 sts, k2.

Rep rows 1–2 twice more.

Change to US size 6 needles.

Row 7: [P1, k1] to last 8 sts, C4B, C4F.

Row 8: P8, [p1, k1] to end of row.

Row 9: [K1, p1] to last 8 sts, k8.

Row 10: P8, [k1, p1] to end of row.

Rep rows 7–10, 3(3:4) times more.

Row 23(23:27): As row 7.

Row 24(24:28): As row 8.

Row 25(25:29): Keeping double seed patt correct as set, patt to last 9 sts, inc, k8. *43(47:51) sts*

Row 26(26:30): P8, patt to end of row.

Row 27(27:31): Patt to last 9 sts, inc, C4B, C4F. *44(48:52) sts*

Row 28(28:32): P8, patt to end of row.

Row 29(29:33): Patt to last 9 sts, inc, k8. *45(49:53) sts*

Row 30(30:34): P8, patt to end of row.

Row 31(31:35): As row 27(27:31). *46(50:54) sts*

Row 32(32:36): As row 28(28:32).

Row 33(33:37): As row 29(29:33). *47(51:55) sts*

Row 34(34:38): P8, patt to end of row.

Right front side

Row 35(35:39): Patt 26(28:30) sts, turn (leave rem 21(23:25) sts on a stitch holder).

Row 36(36:40): Bind off 2 sts, patt to end of row. *24(26:28) sts*

Row 37(37:41): Patt to last 3 sts, k2tog, k1.

Row 38(38:42): P1, p2tog, patt to end of row. *22(24:26) sts*

Rows 39–50(39–50:43–54): Patt to end of row.

Row 51(51:55): Bind off 4 sts (1 st on right-hand needle), ssk, patt to end of row. *17(19:21) sts*

Row 52(52:56): Patt to last 3 sts, p2tog, p1. *16(18:20) sts*

Row 53(53:57): K1, ssk, patt to end of row. *15(17:19) sts*

Row 54(54:58): As row 52(52:56). *14(16:18) sts*
Row 55(55:59): As row 53(53:57). *13(15:17) sts*
Row 56(56:60): As row 52(52:56). *12(14:16) sts*
Row 57(57:61): As row 53(53:57). *11(13:15) sts*

Row 58(58:62): As row 52(52:56). *10(12:14) sts*
Row 59(59:63): As row 53(53:57). *9(11:13) sts*
Rows 60−62(60−62:64−66): Patt to end of row.
Row 63(63:67): Patt 6 sts, turn.
Row 64(64:68): Patt to end of row.
Bind off all sts.

BACK

WS facing, slip rem 21(23:25) sts of the Left Back onto US size 6 needle and re-join yarn.
Bind off 2 sts, keeping double seed patt correct as set, patt to last 8 sts, p8. *19(21:23) sts*
Cast on 11(13:15) sts onto the same needle and cut off a long length of yarn. *30(34:38) sts*
RS facing, slip rem 21(23:25) sts of the Right Back onto the same US size 6 needle. *51(57:63) sts*
Row 35(35:39): Bind off 2 sts, patt 11(13:15) sts including st used to bind off, C4B, C4F, k11(13:15), C4B, C4F, patt to end of row. *49(55:61) sts*
Row 36(36:40): P1, p2tog, work in double seed patt as set to last 3 sts, p2tog, p1. *47(53:59) sts*
Row 37(37:41): K1, ssk, patt to last 3 sts, k2tog, k1. *45(51:57) sts*
Rows 38−62(38−62:42−66): Patt to end of row.
Row 63(63:67): Patt to last 3(5:7) sts, turn.
Row 64(64:68): Patt to last 3(5:7) sts, turn.
Bind off all sts.

Sleeve (make two)

Using US size 3 needles, cast on 40(40:44) sts.
Row 1: [K2, p2] to end of row.
Rep row 1, 5 times more.
Change to US size 6 needles.
Row 7: Bind off 2 sts (1 st on right-hand needle), [p1, k1] to last st, p1. 38(38:42) sts
Row 8: Bind off 2 sts (1 st on right-hand needle), [p1, k1] to last st, p1. 36(36:40) sts
Row 9: K1, ssk, keeping double seed patt correct as set, patt to last 3 sts, k2tog, k1. 34(34:38) sts
Row 10: P2, patt to last 2 sts, p2. 32(32:36) sts
Rep rows 9–10 until there are 28(28:36) sts.
Next row: As row 9. 26(26:34) sts
Next row: P1, p2tog, patt to last 3 sts, p2tog, p1. 24(24:32) sts
Rep last 2 rows until 4 sts rem.
Bind off.

Finishing

Weave in loose ends. Steam the pieces following directions on the yarn label. Join shoulders. Set in sleeves and join sleeve seams.

Front bands
**Using US size 3 needles, pick up 36(36:40) sts along the left front edge.

Row 1: [K2, p2] to end of row.
Rep row 1, 4 times more.
Bind off.**
Rep from ** to ** along right front edge.
Working two rows of crochet along the neckline is an option.

Fabric ruffle
Wash the fabric to prevent it shrinking later. Cut the fabric so it measures 8¾ x 43 (11 x 43:14 x 43) in. Zigzag stitch along all edges. Using an iron, fold and press under a narrow hem on the two short edges and then one long (bottom) edge. Machine hem these edges. Using big running stitches and leaving a long tail of thread at both ends, sew along the top edge. Pull up the thread at both ends to gather the fabric. Even out and adjust the gathers so that the top gathered edge of the ruffle measures 26(26½:27½) in. Measure the width of the cardigan from inside front band to inside front band and, if necessary, adjust the length of the ruffle to fit across it. Sew on the bias binding over the gathered edge. Lastly, hand-sew the fabric onto the wrong side of the cardigan level with the armholes, attaching it to cast on stitches at center back and beginning and ending inside front bands. Sew on snap, button, or hook and eye at neck edge, or use ribbon ties.

Sophia Elf Cardigan with Fabric

Elvira Frost Flower Cardigan

This cardigan got its inspiration from the "Frost Flower" stitch pattern. It is a knit and purl pattern that is not too difficult, but it does require you to stay focused while knitting and counting.

MEASUREMENTS

Size	3–4 yrs
To fit chest	23 in
Finished chest measurement	24 in

YARN

4 x 1¾ oz skeins of Mirasol Sulka in Snow White 200

MATERIALS

Pair each of US size 8 and US size 10 knitting needles
5 stitch holders
Tapestry needle
One large snap

GAUGE

12 sts and 18 rows to 4 in over st st using US size 10 needles

ABBREVIATIONS

See page 140

BACK

Using US size 8 needles, cast on 36 sts.

Row 1: Knit.

Row 2: [K1, p1] to end of row.

Row 3: [P1, k1] to end of row.

Row 4: [K1, p1] to end of row.

Change to US size 10 needles.

Row 5: K4, k2tog, k4, yo, p2, [k2, yo, ssk] 3 times, p2, yo, k4, ssk, k4.

Row 6: P3, p2togtbl, p4, yo, p1, k2, [p2, yo, p2tog] 3 times, k2, p1, yo, p4, p2tog, p3.

Row 7: K2, k2tog, k4, yo, k2, p2, [k2, yo, ssk] 3 times, p2, k2, yo, k4, ssk, k2.

Row 8: P1, p2togtbl, p4, yo, p3, k2, [p2, yo, p2tog] 3 times, k2, p3, yo, p4, p2tog, p1.

Rep rows 5–8 twice more.

Row 17: K1, yo, ssk, k2, yo, ssk, p2, yo, k4, ssk, k6, k2tog, k4, yo, p2, k2, yo, ssk, k3.

Row 18: P1, yo, p2tog, p2, yo, p2tog, k2, p1, yo, p4, p2tog, p4, p2togtbl, p4, yo, p1, k2, p2, yo, p2tog, p3.

Row 19: K1, yo, ssk, k2, yo, ssk, p2, k2, yo, k4, ssk, k2, k2tog, k4, yo, k2, p2, k2, yo, ssk, k3.

Row 20: P1, yo, p2tog, p2, yo, p2tog, k2, p3, yo, p4, p2tog, p2togtbl, p4, yo, p3, k2, p2, yo, p2tog, p3.

Rep rows 17–20 twice more.

Starting with a k row, work 8 rows st st.

Elvira Frost Flower Cardigan

Shape raglan armholes
Rows 37–38: Bind off 2 sts at beg of next 2 rows.
32 sts
Rows 39–52: Dec 1 st at each end of every alt row for 14 rows and dec 1 st at center on last row.
17 sts
Leave 17 sts on a stitch holder.

LEFT FRONT

Using US size 8 needles, cast on 22 sts.
Row 1: Knit.
Row 2: [P1, k1] to end of row.
Row 3: [K1, p1] to end of row.
Row 4: [P1, k1] to end of row.
Change to US size 10 needles.
Row 5: K4, k2tog, k4, yo, p2, k2, yo, ssk, k3, p1, k1, p1.
Row 6: P1, k1, p1, k1, yo, p2tog, p2, yo, p2tog, k2, p1, yo, p4, p2tog, p3.
Row 7: K2, k2tog, k4, yo, k2, p2, k2, yo, ssk, k3, p1, k1, p1.
Row 8: P1, k1, p1, k1, yo, p2tog, p2, yo, p2tog, k2, p3, yo, p4, p2tog, p1.
Rep rows 5–8 twice more.
Row 17: K1, yo, ssk, k2, yo, ssk, p2, yo, k4, ssk, k4, p1, k1, p1.
Row 18: P1, k1, p1, k1, p2, p2togtbl, p4, yo, p1, k2, p2, yo, p2tog, p3.

Row 19: K1, yo, ssk, k2, yo, ssk, p2, k2, yo, k4, ssk, k2, p1, k1, p1.
Row 20: P1, k1, p1, k1, p2togtbl, p4, yo, p3, k2, p2, yo, p2tog, p3.
Rep rows 17–20 twice more.
Row 29: K to last 3 sts, p1, k1, p1.
Row 30: P1, k1, p1, k1, p to end of row.
Rep rows 29–30, 3 times more.
Shape raglan armhole
Row 37: Bind off 2 sts, patt to end of row. *20 sts*
Keeping the seed stitch at front edge correct as set, work 1 row and then dec 1 st at armhole edge on every alt row for 14 rows. *13 sts*
Leave 13 sts on a stitch holder.

RIGHT FRONT

Using US size 8 needles, cast on 22 sts.
Row 1: Knit.
Row 2: [K1, p1] to end of row.
Row 3: [P1, k1] to end of row.
Row 4: [K1, p1] to end of row.
Change to US size 10 needles.
Row 5: P1, k1, p1, k1, yo, ssk, k2, yo, ssk, p2, yo, k4, ssk, k4.
Row 6: P3, p2togtbl, p4, yo, p1, k2, p2, yo, p2tog, p2, k1, p1, k1, p1.
Row 7: P1, k1, p1, k1, yo, ssk, k2, yo, ssk, p2, k2, yo, k4, ssk, k2.

Row 8: P1, p2togtbl, p4, yo, p3, k2, p2, yo, p2tog, p2, k1, p1, k1, p1.
Rep rows 5–8 twice more.
Row 17: P1, k1, p1, k4, k2tog, k4, yo, p2, k2, yo, ssk, k3.
Row 18: P1, yo, p2tog, p2, yo, p2tog, k2, p1, yo, p4, p2tog, p2, k1, p1, k1, p1.
Row 19: P1, k1, p1, k2, k2tog, k4, yo, k2, p2, k2, yo, ssk, k3.
Row 20: P1, yo, p2tog, p2, yo, p2tog, k2, p3, yo, p4, p2tog, k1, p1, k1, p1.
Rep rows 17–20 twice more.
Row 29: P1, k1, p1, k to end of row.
Row 30: P to last 4 sts, k1, p1, k1, p1.
Rep rows 29–30, 3 times more, then rep row 29 once more.

Shape raglan armhole
Row 38: Bind off 2 sts, p to last 4 sts, k1, p1, k1, p1. *20 sts*
Keeping the seed stitch at front edge correct as set, dec 1 st at armhole edge on every alt row for 14 rows. *13 sts*
Leave 13 sts on a stitch holder.

SLEEVE (MAKE TWO)

Using US size 8 needles, cast on 26 sts.
Row 1: Knit.
Row 2: [K1, p1] to end of row.

Row 3: [P1, k1] to end of row.
Row 4: [K1, p1] to end of row.
Change to US size 10 needles.
Shape raglan sleeve top
Dec 1 st at each end on every alt row for next 14 rows. *12 sts*
Leave 12 sts on a stitch holder.

FINISHING

Weave in loose ends.
Steam the pieces following directions on the yarn label.

Neckband
RS facing, slip left front, sleeve, back, sleeve, right front onto a US size 8 needle. *67 sts*
Row 1: [P1, k1] to last st, p1.
Row 2: [K1, p1] to last st, k1.
Row 3: [P1, k1] to last st, p1.
Bind off.

Sew the sleeves to the front and back, joining first 4 rows to bound off stitches underarm. Sew side seams from end of sleeve to lower edge of body. Sew on snap at neck.

Elvira Frost Flower Cardigan

Maggie Grandpa Cardigan

Patience is a virtue: this is one of the bigger garments and does take a while to make. The small cable pattern itself is not hard to learn, although the shaping requires concentration. This cardigan shape is a classic that will last through the seasons.

MEASUREMENTS

Size	3–4 yrs	5–6 yrs	7–8 yrs
To fit chest	23 in	24 in	25¼ in
Finished chest measurement	24½ in	25½ in	27 in
Finished sleeve seam	11 in	12¾ in	15 in

YARN

8(8:9) x 1¾ oz balls of Rowan Lima in Andes 880

MATERIALS

Pair each of US size 4 and US size 8 knitting needles
Cable needle
Tapestry needle

GAUGE

26 sts and 25 rows to 4 in over patt using US size 8 needles

ABBREVIATIONS

C6B—slip next 3 sts onto cable needle and hold at back of work, knit next 3 sts from left-hand needle, then knit 3 sts from cable needle.
See also page 140

CROSSOVER STITCH PATTERN

(Worked over multiple of 10 sts)
Row 1: K2, [C6B, k4] to last 8 sts, C6B, k2.
Row 2 and all even-numbered rows: Purl.
Row 3: *Slip next 2 sts onto cable needle and hold at back of work, k1, k2 from cable needle, yo, skpo, k2tog, yo, slip next 1 st onto cable needle and hold in front of work, k2, k1 from cable needle, rep from * to end of row.
Row 5: K3, [yo, skpo, k2tog, yo, k6] to last 7 sts, yo, skpo, k2tog, yo, k3.
Row 7: K3, [yo, skpo, k2tog, yo, C6B] to last 7 sts, yo, skpo, k2tog, yo, k3.
Row 9: K3, [yo, skpo, k2tog, yo, k6] to last 7 sts, yo, skpo, k2tog, yo, k3.
Row 11: *Slip next 1 st onto cable needle and hold in front of work, k2, k1 from cable needle, yo, skpo, k2tog, yo, slip next 2 sts onto cable needle and hold at back of work, k1, k2 from cable needle, rep from * to end of row.
Row 12: Purl.
Rep these 12 rows.

BACK

Sizes 3–4 and 7–8: Work patt.
Size 5–6: Add 2 edge sts in st st to each side of patt.

Using US size 4 needles, cast on 80(84:88) sts.
Row 1: [K2, p2] to end of row.
Rep row 1, 7 times more, inc 1 st at each end of last row on size 7–8. *80(84:90) sts*
Change to US size 8 needles.
Work crossover patt for 72(84:96) rows.
Shape raglan armholes
Row 81(93:105): Bind off 2 sts, patt to end of row. *78(82:88) sts*
Row 82(94:106): Bind off 2 sts, p to end of row. *76(80:86) sts*
Keeping patt correct as set, dec 1 st at each end of every 4th row for 24 rows. *Row 106(118:130) completed; 64(68:74) sts*
Keeping patt correct as set, dec 1 st at each end of every row for 12 rows. *Row 118(130:142) completed; 52(56:62) sts*
Bind off.

LEFT FRONT

Sizes 3–4 and 7–8: Work patt.
Size 5–6: Add 2 edge sts to each side of patt.
Using US size 4 needles, cast on 34(40:40) sts.
Row 1: [K2, p2] to end of row.
Rep row 1, 7 times more.
Change to US size 8 needles.
Work crossover patt for 58(62:74) rows.
Row 66(70:82) completed

Maggie Grandpa Cardigan

Shape front edge

Keeping patt correct as set, dec 1 st at end of next and at same edge of every 3rd row for 14(22:22) rows. *Row 80(92:104) completed; 29(32:32) sts*

Shape raglan armhole

Row 81(93:105) (RS): Bind off 2 sts, patt to end of row. *27(30:30) sts*

Row 82(94:106): Dec 1 st for size 3–4 only, purl to end of row. *26(30:30) sts*

Keeping patt correct as set, cont to dec 1 st at neck edge as set on 3rd rows for 24(4:4) rows, then dec 1 st on alt rows for 10(30:30) rows, **at the same time** dec 1 st at armhole edge on 4th rows for 24 rows, then on alt rows for 10 rows. *Row 116(128:140) completed; 2 sts*

Work 1 row.

Next row: K2tog and fasten off.

Right front

Sizes 3–4 and 7–8: Work patt.

Size 5–6: Add 2 edge sts to each side of patt.

Using US size 4 needles, cast on 34(40:40) sts.

Row 1: [K2, p2] to end of row.

Rep row 1, 7 times more.

Change to US size 8 needles.

Work crossover patt for 58(62:74) rows. *Row 66(70:82) completed*

Shape front edge

Keeping patt correct as set, dec 1 st at beg of next and at same edge of every 3rd row for 15(23:23) rows. *Row 81(93:105) completed; 29(32:32) sts*

Shape raglan armhole

Row 82(94:106) (WS): Bind off 2 sts, purl to end of row dec 1 st for size 3–4. *26(30:30) sts*

Keeping patt correct as set, cont to dec 1 st at neck edge as set on 3rd rows for 24(4:4) rows, then dec 1 st on alt rows for 10(30:30) rows, **at the same time** dec 1 st at armhole edge on 4th rows for 24 rows, then on alt rows for 10 rows. *Row 116(128:140) completed; 2 sts*

Work 1 row.

Next row: K2tog and fasten off.

Right sleeve

***Sizes 3–4 and 7–8:* Work patt.

Size 5–6: Add 1 edge st in st st to each side of patt.

Using US size 4 needles, cast on 40(40:48) sts.

Row 1: [K2, p2] to end of row.

Rep row 1, 7 times more, and on last row inc 1 st at each end on sizes 5–6 and 7–8. *40(42:50) sts*

Change to US size 8 needles.

Work crossover patt, **at the same time** inc 1 st at each end of every 9th row until there are 52(56:68) sts.

Work 10(11:5) rows even.

Shape raglan sleeve top

Row 69(81:93): Bind off 2 sts, patt to end of row. *50(54:66) sts*

Row 70(82:94): Bind off 2 sts, p to end of row. *48(52:64) sts*

Keeping patt correct as set, dec 1 st at each end of every 3rd row for 24 rows. *Row 94(106:118) completed; 32(36:48) sts*

Keeping patt correct as set, dec 1 st at each end on every row for 12 rows.** *Row 106(118:130) completed; 8(12:24) sts*

Sizes 5–6 and 7–8 only

Row 119(131): Bind off (2:14) sts. *(10:10) sts rem*

All sizes

Starting with a k(p:p) row, work 7(9:11) rows st st.

Bind off.

LEFT SLEEVE

Work as for Right Sleeve from ** to **.

Sizes 5–6 and 7–8 only

Row 119(131): Patt to end of row.

Row 120(132): Bind off (2:14) sts. *(10:10) sts rem*

All sizes

Starting with a k row, work 7(9:11) rows st st.

Bind off.

Weave in loose ends.

Steam the pieces following directions on the yarn label.

Sew together the two sleeves at the top narrow ends, which will meet at the back of the neck. Then sew in the back piece so that the center top meets the two narrow sleeve ends (you may need to gather the center back, but that will just add a bit of character).

Sew the front part of the sleeves to the front parts of the body.

Front band

Using US size 4 needles and with RS facing, pick up 90(110:140) sts from lower right front edge to center back and 90(110:140) sts down to lower left front edge. *Total of 180:220:280 sts*

Row 1: [K2, p2] to end of row.

Rep row 1, 6 times more.

Bind off.

(I worked the two sides separately and joined the two ribs at the back of the neck afterwards as this is a lot of stitches to work with at once.)

Sew up the underarm and side seams from end of sleeve to lower edge of body.

Maggie Grandpa Cardigan

Marie Cardigan with Lace Edges

This lacy project also looks terrific with the main cardigan knit in stockinette stitch and decorated with a sewn-on lace edge. If you choose to do this, just cast on fewer stitches at the start.

MEASUREMENTS

Size	3–4 yrs	5–6 yrs	7–8 yrs
To fit chest	23 in	24 in	25¼ in
Finished chest measurement	23 in	23 in	28¼ in
Finished sleeve seam	7¼ in	8¼ in	9¼ in

Note: Finished chest measurement for 3–4 years and 5–6 years is the same and should easily fit both.

YARN

5(5:6) x 1¾ oz balls of Garnstudio Drops Alpaca in Light Grey 0501 used DOUBLE throughout

MATERIALS

Pair each of US size 3 and US size 6 knitting needles
Cable needle
Tapestry needle
3 x 1 in buttons
Sewing needle and thread

GAUGE

20 sts and 24 rows to 4 in over patt using US size 6 needles and two strands of yarn held together

See page 140

LACE PATTERN

(7 sts to 8 sts to 9 sts, plus 2 edge sts—note that the number of sts alternates)
Row 1 (RS): K1, [k6, p1, yo] to last st, k1.
Row 2 and all even-numbered rows: Work sts in patt and purl yarnovers.
Row 3: K1, [k6, p2, yo] to last st, k1.
Row 5: K1, [slip next 3 sts onto cable needle and hold at back of work, k3tog from left-hand needle, k3 from cable needle, p3] to last st, k1.
Row 7: K1, [yo, p1, k6] to last st, k1.
Row 9: K1, [yo, p2, k6] to last st, k1.
Row 11: K1, [p3, slip next 3 sts onto cable needle and hold in front of work, k3, k3togtbl from cable needle] to last st, k1.
Row 12: Work sts in patt.
Rep these 12 rows.

BACK

Using US size 6 needles and 2 strands of yarn, cast on 58(58:72) sts.
Row 1: Purl.

Starting with patt row 1 (RS), work 36(42:48) rows in patt.
Shape armholes
Keeping patt correct as set, bind off 2 sts at each end of next 2 rows. *54(54:68) sts*
Dec 1 st at each end of next 2 rows. *50(50:64) sts*
Work 26(26:32) rows in patt.
Next row: Bind off 12(12:14) sts, patt to end of row.
Next row: Bind off 12(12:14) sts, patt to end of row.
Bind off.

LEFT FRONT

Using US size 6 needles and 2 strands of yarn, cast on 9(9:16) sts.
Row 1: Purl.
Starting with patt row 7 (RS), work 12 rows in patt, **at the same time** inc 1 st at front edge of every row. *21(21:28) sts*
Keeping patt correct as set, work 8 rows in patt, **at the same time** inc 1 st at front edge of every alt row. *25(25:32) sts*
Keeping patt correct as set, cont until you have worked 36(42:48) rows in patt.
Shape armhole
Next row (RS): Bind off 2 sts, patt to end of row.
Dec 1 st at armhole edge on next 2 rows.
21(21:28) sts
Work 14(14:20) rows in patt.

Marie Cardigan with Lace Edges

Shape neck

Next row (WS): Bind off 9(9:14) sts, patt to end of row. *12(12:14) sts*

Work 12 rows in patt.

Bind off.

RIGHT FRONT

Using US size 6 needles and 2 strands of yarn, cast on 9(9:16) sts.

Row 1: Purl.

Starting with patt row 7 (RS), work 12 rows in patt, **at the same time** inc 1 st at front edge of every row. *21(21:28) sts*

Keeping patt correct as set, work 8 rows in patt, **at the same time** inc 1 st at front edge of every alt row. *25(25:32) sts*

Keeping patt correct as set, cont until you have worked 37(43:49) rows in patt.

Shape armhole

Next row (WS): Bind off 2 sts, patt to end of row. *23(23:30) sts*

Dec 1 st at armhole edge on next 2 rows. *21(21:28) sts*

Work 14(14:20) rows in patt.

Shape neck

Next row (RS): Bind off 9(9:14) sts. *12(12:14) sts*

Work 12 rows in patt.

Bind off.

SLEEVE (MAKE TWO)

Using US size 6 needles and 2 strands of yarn, cast on 37 sts.

Row 1: Purl.

Cont in patt, **at the same time** inc 1 st at each end of every 8th(10th:4th) row until there are 43(43:45) sts.

Work 6(6:6) rows even.

Shape sleeve top

Bind off 2 sts at beg of next 2 rows. *39(39:51) sts*

Keeping patt correct as set, dec 1 st at each end of every row for next 10(10:12) rows. *19(19:27) sts*

Bind off 2 sts at beg of every row for 6(6:10) rows. *7(7:7) sts*

Bind off.

NECKBAND

Sew up the shoulder seams.

Using US size 3 needles and 2 strands of yarn and with RS facing, pick up 62(62:72) sts around the edges of the neck.

Row 1: [K1, p1] to end of row.

Rep row 1, 3 times more.

Bind off.

LACE RIBBON EDGE TRIM

Using US size 6 needles and 2 strands of yarn, cast on 8 sts.

Row 1: Knit.
Row 2: K1, [yo, p2tog] twice, yo, k3.
Row 3: K4, [yo, p2tog] twice, k1.
Row 4: K1, [yo, p2tog] twice, yo, k4.
Row 5: K5, [yo, p2tog] twice, k1.
Row 6: K1, [yo, p2tog] twice, yo, k5.
Row 7: K6, [yo, p2tog] twice, k1.
Row 8: K1, [yo, p2tog] twice, yo, k6.
Row 9: K7, [yo, p2tog] twice, k1.
Row 10: K1, [yo, p2tog] twice, yo, k7.
Row 11: K8, [yo, p2tog] twice, k1.
Row 12: K1, [yo, p2tog] twice, k8.
Row 13: Bind off 6 sts, k3 including st used to bind off, [yo, p2tog] twice, k1.
Rep rows 2–13 about 27(28:29) times, or until you have enough ribbon to go around the front and back edges of the cardigan.
Bind off.

SLEEVE TRIM (MAKE TWO)

Work rows 1–13 of lace ribbon edge trim, then rep rows 2–13, 5 times.
Bind off.

FINISHING

Weave in loose ends.
Press the pieces following directions on the yarn label.
Sew up the shoulder seams.
Sew the lace trim to the sleeve cuffs, then sew the sleeves to the body.
Sew up the underarm and side seams from end of sleeve to lower edge of body.
Pin the lace trim evenly around the edge of the cardigan and sew it in place.
Sew on buttons evenly spaced on left front edge trim and use lace holes in right front edge trim as buttonholes.

Marie Cardigan with Lace Edges

Rosita Warm-wrap Cardigan

Wrap yourself in patience before starting this project. I like
to think that the labor put into this piece will make it last
longer—at least a few years if you make it in a good size. It
is a lovely cardigan to have for a cozy Sunday morning,
but it also works well as a jacket for the fall. This pattern
looks great as a vest, too: simply knit the body and leave
off the sleeves.

MEASUREMENTS

Size	3–4 yrs	5–6 yrs	7–8 yrs
To fit chest	23 in	24 in	25¼ in
Finished measurement across back	9½ in	10¼ in	11¾ in
Finished sleeve seam	11 in	12 in	12¾ in

YARN

8(8:9) x 1¾ oz balls of Rowan by Amy Butler Belle Organic Aran in
Moonflower 208

MATERIALS

Pair of US size 7 knitting needles
Cable needle
Tapestry needle
Approx 52 in of 1 in ribbon for the tie
Sewing needle and thread

GAUGE

22 sts and 22 rows to 4 in over patt using US size 7 needles

ABBREVIATIONS

C3B—slip next 2 sts onto cable needle and hold at back of work, knit next 1 st from left-hand needle, then knit 2 sts from cable needle.

C3F—slip next 1 st onto cable needle and hold in front of work, knit next 2 sts from left-hand needle, then knit 1 st from cable needle.

See also page 140

Note: The front and back are knitted in one, starting from the back neck, knitting around the body, and ending at the back neck. As the garment is sewn up in a visible place at the back, it is important to sew it with mattress stitch for an invisible seam.

BODY

Part one

Cast on 41(55:55) sts for left front section, beg at center back neck.

Row 1: Purl.

Row 2 (RS): [C3B, C3F, p1] 5(7:7) times, C3B, C3F.

Row 3: [P6, k1] 2(4:4) times, p6, turn.

Row 4: [C3B, C3F, p1] 2(4:4) times (when working the first C3B, slip the 2 sts onto the cable needle, then pick up a loop from the previous row and work tog with first st so as not to leave a gap), C3B, C3F.

Sizes 5–6 and 7–8 only

Row 5: P6, k1, p6, turn.

Row 6: C3B, C3F, p1 (when working the first C3B, slip the 2 sts onto the cable needle, then pick up a loop from the previous row and work tog with first st so as not to leave a gap), C3B, C3F.

All sizes

Row 5(7:7): [P6, k1] 5(7:7) times, p6.

Rep rows 2–5(2–7:2–7), 20(22:24) times more. Having worked the last row of the last rep, cast on a further 29 sts onto the same needle for the left back armhole edge. *70(84:84) sts*

Part two

Start part two, reversing patt for back section.

Row 1 (RS): [K1, p6] 10(12:12) times.

Row 2: [C3B, C3F, p1] 10(12:12) times.

Row 3: [K1, p6] 10(12:12) times.

Row 4: [C3B, C3F, p1] 3(5:5) times, turn.

Row 5: K1, [p6, k1] 2(4:4) times, p6 (when working the first knit stitch, knit it together with a loop from the previous row so as not to leave a gap between sts).

Sizes 5–6 and 7–8 only

Row 6: C3B, C3F, p1, C3B, C3F, turn.

Row 7: P6, k1, p6 (when working the first purl stitch, purl it together with a loop from the previous row so as not to leave a gap between sts).

All sizes

Rep rows 2–5(2–7:2–7), 24(26:28) times more, then rep row 2 once more.

Rosita Warm Wrap Cardigan

Next row (RS): Bind off 29 sts for right back armhole edge, patt (row 3) to end of row. *41(55:55) sts*

Part three

Start part three, reversing patt for right front section.

Row 1: [P6, k1] 5(7:7) times, p6.

Row 2 (RS): [C3B, C3F, p1] 5(7:7) times, C3B, C3F.

Row 3: [P6, k1] 2(4:4) times, p6, turn.

Row 4: [C3B, C3F, p1] 2(4:4) times (when working the first C3B, slip the 2 sts onto the cable needle, then pick up a loop from the previous row and work tog with first st so as not to leave a gap), C3B, C3F.

Sizes 5–6 and 7–8 only

Row 5: P6, k1, p6, turn.

Row 6: C3B, C3F, p1 (when working the first C3B, slip the 2 sts onto the cable needle then pick up a loop from the previous row and work tog with first st so as not to leave a gap), C3B, C3F.

All sizes

Row 5(7:7): [P6, k1] 5(7:7) times, p6.

Rep rows 2–5(2–7:2–7), 20(22:24) times more, binding off on the last row of the last rep.

When binding off, work [k1, k2tog, k2, k2tog] across the row to create a more even edge.

Sleeve (make two)

Cast on 36 sts.
Rows 1–3: [K1, p1] to end of row.
Row 4: [P1, C3B, C3F] 5 times, p1.
Row 5: [K1, p6] 5 times, k1.
Rows 4–5 form the sleeve patt.
Keeping patt correct as set, shape as folls:
Work 60(64:68) rows, **at the same time** inc and
work into patt 1 st at each end of every 10th row
until there are 48 sts.
Bind off 2 sts at beg of next 2 rows. *44 sts*
Dec 1 st at each end of every row for next 10 rows.
24 sts
Bind off, working [k1, k2tog] across the row to
create a more even edge.

Finishing

Weave in loose ends.
Press the pieces following directions on the
yarn label.
Join the cast on and bound off edges with an
invisible seam for back neck. Mark the center of
the back at the row edge. Place this point to
center back neck and sew the inner circle to the
back to form shoulders. Join the sleeves to the
now closed armholes, easing to fit, and sew
together, then sew the sides of the sleeves. Cut
the ribbon in half and sew a length to each side
just under the armholes to tie at the front.

Rosita Warm Wrap Cardigan

Dresses and Tops

Penelope Garter Stitch Vest

This is great if you are looking for something basic to knit, but stylish to wear. It merely requires that you can do garter stitch and a bit of shaping. Although the yarn is thick, the piece is great for layering because it is sleeveless and short.

MEASUREMENTS

Size	3–4 yrs	5–6 yrs	7–8 yrs
To fit chest	23 in	24 in	25¼ in
Finished chest measurement	23½ in	24½ in	26¼ in

YARN

3(3:4) x 1¾ oz skeins of Mirasol Miski in Snowdrop 100

MATERIALS

Pair each of US size 6 and US size 8 knitting needles
Long stitch holder
Tapestry needle
H/8 crochet hook
Approx 20 in of 1 in ribbon (such as grosgrain) for the tie
Sewing needle and thread

GAUGE

15 sts and 32 rows to 4 in over garter stitch using US size 8 needles

Penelope Garter Stitch Vest

See page 140

Note: This is knitted in one piece so that there aren't any seams at the sides.

BEG AT LOWER EDGE OF FRONTS AND BACK

Using US size 6 needles, cast on 112(116:124) sts.
Row 1: Knit.
Change to US size 8 needles.
Cont in garter stitch (knit every row) until work measures 3(3½:4) in from cast on edge, ending with a WS row.
Back gather
Next row: K40(42:46), [k4tog] 8 times, k40(42:46). *88(92:100) sts*
Knit 3 rows.

RIGHT FRONT

Shape armhole
Next row (RS): K21(22:24), turn (leave rem sts on a stitch holder).
Next row: Bind off 2 sts, k to end of row. *19(20:22) sts*
Next row: K to last 2 sts, k2tog. *18(19:21) sts*

Next row: Knit.
Next row: K to last 2 sts, k2tog. *17(18:20) sts*
Knit 19(21:23) rows.
Next row: Bind off 5 sts (1 st on right-hand needle), dec, k to end of row. *11(12:14) sts*
Next row: K to last 3 sts, k2tog, k1. *10(11:13) sts*
Next row: K1, dec, k to end of row. *9(10:12) sts*
Next row: Knit.
Next row: K1, dec, k to end of row. *8(9:11) sts*
Knit 5 rows.
Shape shoulder
Next row (RS): K5(6:6), turn. *3(3:5) sts rem*
Next row: K5(6:6).
Bind off all sts.

BACK

Shape armholes
RS facing, slip 46(48:52) sts from the stitch holder onto the left-hand needle (leave rem 21(22:24) sts on the stitch holder).
Bind off 2 sts at beg of next 2 rows. *42(44:48) sts*
Dec 1 st at each end of next and foll alt row. *38(40:44) sts*
Knit 29(31:33) rows, ending with a WS row.
Shape shoulders
Bind off 3(3:5) sts at beg of next 2 rows and 5(6:6) sts at beg of foll 2 rows.
Bind off rem 22(22:22) sts.

Left front

Shape armhole
RS facing, slip rem 21(22:24) sts from the stitch holder onto the left-hand needle.
Next row: Bind off 2 sts, k to end of row. *19(20:22) sts*
Next row: Knit.
Next row: Dec, k to end of row. *18(19:21) sts*
Next row: Knit.
Next row: Dec, k to end of row. *17(18:20) sts*
Knit 18(20:22) rows, ending with a RS row.
Next row: Bind off 5 sts (1 st on right-hand needle), dec, k to end of row. *11(12:14) sts*
Next row: K to last 3 sts, dec, k1. *10(11:13) sts*
Next row: K1, dec, k to end of row. *9(10:12) sts*
Next row: Knit.
Next row: K1, dec, k to end of row. *8(9:11) sts*
Knit 5 rows.
Shape shoulder
Next row (WS): K5(6:6), turn. *3(3:5) sts rem*
Next row: K5(6:6).
Bind off all sts.

Finishing

Weave in loose ends.
Steam the pieces following directions on the yarn label.
Sew up the shoulder seams.
Work single crochet edge around the sides. Cut the ribbon in half and sew a length to each side of the top front center and tie in a bow.

Penelope Garter Stitch Waistcoat

Holly Warm Loopy Vest

This is a cozy garment to have when it is cold and it can also be used as an outerwear piece in spring. Once you get into the loop technique it is not a difficult piece to make, and it gives a more natural look if the loops are not completely the same length. To create the dense "furry" texture, the loops are knitted on every stitch.

MEASUREMENTS

Size	3–4 yrs	5–6 yrs	7–8 yrs
To fit chest	23 in	24 in	25¼ in
Finished chest measurement	24 in	25¼ in	26½ in

YARN

2 x 3½ oz balls of Rowan Drift in Sombre 903
Note: Depending how long you make the loops, you may need more yarn.

MATERIALS

Pair of US size 11 knitting needles
Tapestry needle
Approx 20 in of 1 in ribbon for the tie
Sewing needle and thread

GAUGE

9 sts and 13 rows to 4 in over patt using US 11 needles

ML—make loop: k1, keeping st on left-hand needle, bring yarn forward, pass yarn over left thumb to make a loop (approx 1½–2 in), take yarn to the back, knit stitch again, slip st off left-hand needle, yo and pass the 2 sts just worked over this loop.
See also page 140

KNITTED IN ONE PIECE

Cast on 39(41:45) sts.
Bottom section
Row 1: Purl.
Row 2 (RS): K1, inc and ML from this st, [ML] to last 2 sts, inc and ML from this st, k1. *41(43:47) sts*
Row 3: P1, inc, p to last 2 sts, inc, p1. *43(45:49) sts*
Row 4: As row 2. *45(47:51) sts*
Row 5: As row 3. *47(49:53) sts*
Row 6: K1, [ML] to last st, k1.
Row 7: P1, inc, p to last 2 sts, inc, p1. *49(51:55) sts*
Row 8: As row 6.
Row 9: As row 7. *51(53:57) sts*

RIGHT FRONT

Row 10: K1, [ML] 11(11:12) times, turn (leave rem sts on a stitch holder).
Row 11: Bind off 1 st, p to end of row. *11(11:12) sts*
Row 12: K1, [ML] 7(7:8) times, k2tog and ML from this st, k1. *10(10:11) sts*
Row 13: P1, p2tog, p to end of row. *9(9:10) sts*
Row 14: K1, inc and ML from this st, [ML] to last 3 sts, k2tog and ML from this st, k1. *9(9:10) sts*
Row 15: Purl.
Row 16: [ML] to end of row.
Rep rows 15–16, 3 times more.
Row 23: Purl.
Shape neck
Row 24: **At the same time** as making a loop in the sts, bind off 2 sts (1 st on right-hand needle), k2tog and ML from this st, [ML] to last st, k1. *6(6:7) sts*
Row 25: P to last 3 sts, p2tog, p1. *5(5:6) sts*
Row 26: K1, k2tog and ML from this st, [ML] to last st, k1. *4(4:5) sts*
Row 27: Purl.
Row 28: K1, [ML] to end of row.
Shape shoulder
Row 29: Bind off 2 sts, p to end of row. *2(2:3) sts*
Bind off the sts, making a loop in each before binding them off.

Holly Warm Loopy Vest

BACK

Slip the next 27(29:31) sts from the stitch holder onto needle.

Row 10 (RS): Bind off 1 st, [ML] to last st, k1. *26(28:30) sts*

Row 11: Bind off 1 st, p to end of row. *25(27:29) sts*

Row 12: K1, k2tog and ML from this st, [ML] to last 3 sts, k2tog and ML from this st, k1. *23(25:27) sts*

Row 13: P1, p2tog, p to last 3 sts, p2tog, p1. *21(23:25) sts*

Row 14: As row 12. *19(21:23) sts*

Row 15: Purl.

Row 16: [ML] to end of row.

Row 17: Purl.

Row 18: As row 12. *17(19:21) sts*

Row 19: Purl.

Row 20: [ML] to end of row.

Rep rows 19–20, 3 times more.

Row 27: Purl.

Shape shoulders

Row 28: Bind off 2 sts, [ML] to end of row. *15(17:19) sts*

Row 29: Bind off 2 sts, p to end of row. *13(15:17) sts*

Bind off the sts, making a loop in each before binding them off.

Left front

Slip rem 12(12:13) sts from the stitch holder onto needle.

Row 10 (RS): Bind off 1 st, [ML] to last st, k1. *11(11:12) sts*

Row 11: Purl.

Row 12: K1, k2tog and ML from this st, [ML] to last st, k1. *10(10:11) sts*

Row 13: P to last 3 sts, p2tog, p1. *9(9:10) sts*

Row 14: K1, k2tog and ML from this st, [ML] to last st, inc and ML from this st, k1. *9(9:10) sts*

Row 15: Purl.

Row 16: [ML] to end of row.

Rep rows 15–16, 3 times more.

Shape neck

Row 23: Bind off 2 sts, p to end of row. *7(7:8) sts*

Row 24: K1, [ML] to last 3 sts, k2tog and ML from this st, k1. *6(6:7) sts*

Row 25: P1, p2tog, p to end of row. *5(5:6) sts*

Row 26: K1, [ML] to last 3 sts, k2tog and ML from this st, k1. *4(4:5) sts*

Row 27: Purl.

Shape shoulder

Row 28: Bind off 2 sts, [ML] to end of row. *2(2:3) sts*

Row 29: Purl.

Bind off the sts, making a loop in each before binding them off.

Finishing

Weave in loose ends.

Steam the pieces on the wrong side following directions on the yarn label.

Sew up shoulder seams.

Cut the ribbon in half and sew on a length at each side of the neckline for the tie.

Holly Warm Loopy Vest

Bertha Shoulder Wrap

A vintage look that's very pretty, and the wrap is reversible.
It would also be lovely if knitted up in a few strands of
mohair, just be sure to work a gauge swatch first.

MEASUREMENTS

Size   one size
Finished measurements   10 x 43 in all around lower edge

YARN

4 x 1¾ oz balls of Louisa Harding Millais in Cottage Rose 02

MATERIALS

24 in US size 8 circular needle
Tapestry needle
Ribbon or button to close (if using a button, then use a crochet hook to make
a little loop)
Sewing needle and thread

GAUGE

14 sts and 20 rows to 4 in over st st using US size 8 needle

ABBREVIATIONS

yo2—yarn over needle twice.
See also page 140

Knitted in One Piece

Cast on 190 sts.

Working back and forth in rows, knit 2 rows.

Row 3: [K1, yo2, ssk, k13, k2tog, yo2, k1] to end of row. *210 sts*

Row 4: [K2, p1, k15, p1, k2] to end of row.

Rows 5–6: Knit.

Row 7: *K1, [yo2, ssk] twice, k11, [k2tog, yo2] twice, k1, rep from * to end of row. *250 sts*

Row 8: *[K2, p1] twice, k13, [p1, k2] twice, rep from * to end of row.

Row 9: Knit.

Row 10: *K6, [yo2, k1] 14 times, k5, rep from * to end of row. *530 sts*

Row 11: *K1, [yo2, ssk] twice, yo2, dropping extra yos from previous row p15 together, yo2, [k2tog, yo2] twice, k1, rep from * to end of row. *190 sts*

Row 12: *K1, [p1, k1] 4 times, k1, [k1, p1] 4 times, k1, rep from * to end of row.

Row 13: Purl.

Row 14: Knit.

Rows 15–16: As rows 13–14.

Row 17: Purl.

Row 18: K1, [k1, k3tog] to last st, k1. *96 sts*

Rows 19–40: Knit.

Row 41: K2, [k2tog] to last 2 sts, k2. *50 sts*

Rows 42–58: Knit.

Bind off all sts.

Finishing

Weave in loose ends.

Steam the pieces following directions on the yarn label.

Either sew on some ribbon to tie the wrap, or make a little loop with a crochet hook and sew on a pretty button to align with it.

Bertha Shoulder Wrap

Isabel Cable and Little Branch Dress

A knitted dress is a great combination of staying warm and the ultimate in comfort, as it never feels tight anywhere. If you would rather make this design as a sweater, it is easy to adjust. Just work as described here and shorten the length to your preferred size.

MEASUREMENTS

Size	3–4 yrs	5–6 yrs	7–8 yrs
To fit chest	22¾ in	24 in	25¼ in
Finished chest measurement	23¾ in	25¾ in	26¾ in
Finished length from armhole to hem	15¼ in	16½ in	17 in

YARN

5(6:6) x 1¾ oz balls of Rowan by Amy Butler Belle Organic DK in Zinc 017

MATERIALS

Pair each of US size 3 and US size 6 knitting needles
2 cable needles
4 stitch holders
Tapestry needle

GAUGE

25 sts and 30 rows to 4 in over patt using US size 6 needles

MB—make bobble: (k1, p1, k1, p1) all into next st, turn, p4, turn, k4, pass 2nd, 3rd and 4th sts over last st on right-hand needle.

C5B—slip next 3 sts onto cable needle and hold at back of work, knit next 2 sts, slip last stitch from cable needle back onto left-hand needle and purl this st, then knit 2 sts from cable needle.

C5F—slip next 2 sts onto cable needle and hold in front of work, slip 1 st onto 2nd cable needle and hold at back, knit next 2 sts, purl 1 st from 2nd cable needle, then knit 2 sts from first cable needle.

C6B—slip next 3 sts onto cable needle and hold at back of work, knit next 3 sts from left-hand needle, then knit 3 sts from cable needle.

C6F—slip next 3 sts onto cable needle and hold in front of work, knit next 3 sts from left-hand needle, then knit 3 sts from cable needle.

C10B—slip next 5 sts onto cable needle and hold at back of work, knit next 5 sts from left-hand needle, then knit 5 sts from cable needle.

C10F—slip next 5 sts onto cable needle and hold in front of work, knit next 5 sts from left-hand needle, then knit 5 sts from cable needle.

C6BP—slip next 3 sts onto cable needle and hold at back of work, knit next 3 sts from left-hand needle, then purl 3 sts from cable needle.

C6FP—slip next 3 sts onto cable needle and hold

Isabel Cable and Little Branch Dress

in front of work, purl next 3 sts from left-hand needle, then knit 3 sts from cable needle.

See also page 140

BACK

Using US size 3 needles, cast on 76(84:88) sts.
Row 1: [K2, p2] to end of row.
Rep row 1, 7 times more.
Change to US size 6 needles.
Row 9: P3(7:9), k10, p2, k12, p2, k3, p3, k6, p3, k3, p2, k12, p2, k10, p3(7:9).
Row 10 and every alt row: Knit purl sts and purl knit sts of previous row.
Row 11: P3(7:9), k10, p2, k12, p2, k3, p3, C6B, p3, k3, p2, k12, p2, k10, p3(7:9).
Row 13: P3(7:9), C10B, p2, C6B, C6F, p2, k3, p3, k6, p3, k3, p2, C6B, C6F, p2, C10F, p3(7:9).
Row 15: P3(7:9), k10, p2, k12, p2, k3, p3, C6B, p3, k3, p2, k12, p2, k10, p3(7:9).
Row 17: P3(7:9), k10, p2, k12, p2, k3, C6BP, C6FP, k3, p2, k12, p2, k10, p3(7:9).
Row 19: P3(7:9), C10B, p2, C6B, C6F, p2, C6B, p6, C6F, p2, C6B, C6F, p2, C10F, p3(7:9).
Row 21: P3(7:9), k10, p2, k12, p2, k3, C6FP, C6BP, k3, p2, k12, p2, k10, p3(7:9).
Row 23: P3(7:9), k10, p2, k12, p2, k3, p3, C6B, p3, k3, p2, k12, p2, k10, p3(7:9).
Row 25: P3(7:9), C10B, p2, C6B, C6F, p2, k3, p3, k6, p3, k3, p2, C6B, C6F, p2, C10F, p3(7:9).

Row 27: P3(7:9), k10, p2, k12, p2, k3, p3, C6B, p3, k3, p2, k12, p2, k10, p3(7:9).
Row 29: P3(7:9), k10, p2, k12, p2, k3, C6BP, C6FP, k3, p2, k12, p2, k10, p3(7:9).
Row 31: P3(7:9), C10B, p2, C6B, C6F, p2, C6B, p6, C6F, p2, C6B, C6F, p2, C10F, p3(7:9).
Row 32: Knit purl sts and purl knit sts of previous row as they appear.
Rep rows 9–32 until work measures 15¼(16½:17) in from cast on edge, ending with a WS row.

Shape raglan armholes
Keeping patt correct as set, shape as folls:
Bind off 2 sts at beg of next 2 rows. *72(80:84) sts*
Dec 1 st at each end of every alt row for 30 rows. *42(50:54) sts*
Leave sts on a stitch holder.

FRONT

Using US size 3 needles, cast on 72(80:84) sts.
Row 1: [K2, p2] to end of row.
Rep row 1, 7 times more.
Change to US size 6 needles.
Row 9: P4(8:10), k10, p6, k2, p1, k2, p2, k3, p3, k6, p3, k3, p2, k2, p1, k2, p6, k10, p4(8:10).
Row 10 and every alt row: Knit purl sts and purl knit sts, knit bobble sts.
Row 11: P4(8:10), k10, p6, k2, p1, k2, p2, k3, p3, C6B, p3, k3, p2, k2, p1, k2, p6, k10, p4(8:10).

Row 13: P4(8:10), C10B, p6, k2, p1, k2, p2, k3, p3, k6, p3, k3, p2, k2, p1, k2, p6, C10F, p4(8:10).
Row 15: P4(8:10), k10, p6, k2, p1, k2, p2, k3, p3, C6B, p3, k3, p2, k2, p1, k2, p6, k10, p4(8:10).
Row 17: P4(8:10), k10, p6, k2, p1, MB, k1, MB, p1, k3, C6BP, C6FP, k3, p1, MB, k1, MB, p1, k2, p6, k10, p4(8:10).
Row 19: P4(8:10), C10B, p3, C5B, p2, MB, p2, C6B, p6, C6F, p2, MB, p2, C5F, p3, C10F, p4(8:10).
Row 21: P4(8:10), k10, p3, k2, p1, k2, p5, k3, C6FP, C6BP, k3, p5, k2, p1, k2, p3, k10, p4(8:10).
Row 23: P4(8:10), k10, p3, k2, p1, k2, p5, k3, p3, C6B, p3, k3, p5, k2, p1, k2, p3, k10, p4(8:10).
Row 25: P4(8:10), C10B, p3, k2, p1, k2, p5, k3, p3, k6, p3, k3, p5, k2, p1, k2, p3, C10F, p4(8:10).
Row 27: P4(8:10), k10, p3, k2, p1, k2, p5, k3, p3, C6B, p3, k3, p5, k2, p1, k2, p3, k10, p4(8:10).
Row 29: P4(8:10), k10, p2, MB, k1, MB, p1, k2, p5, k3, C6BP, C6FP, k3, p5, k2, p1, MB, k1, MB, p2, k10, p4(8:10).
Row 31: P4(8:10), C10B, p3, MB, p2, C5F, p2, C6B, p6, C6F, p2, C5B, p2, MB, p3, C10F, p4(8:10).
Row 32: Knit purl sts and purl knit sts of previous row as they appear, knit bobble sts.
Rep rows 9–32 until work measures 15¼(16½:17) in from cast on edge.

Shape raglan armholes
Keeping patt correct as set, shape as folls:
Bind off 2 sts at beg of next 2 rows. *68(76:80) sts*

Isabel Cable and Little Branch Dress

Dec 1 st at each end of every alt row for 30 rows.
38(46:50) sts
Leave sts on a stitch holder.

Sleeve (make two)

Stitch pattern
Row 1 (RS): P2(4:6), C10B, p5, C6B, p6, C6F, p5, C10F, p2(4:6).
Row 2 and every alt row: Knit purl sts and purl knit sts of previous row.
Row 3: P2(4:6), k10, p5, k3, C6FP, C6BP, k3, p5, k10, p2(4:6).
Row 5: P2(4:6), k10, p5, k3, p3, C6B, p3, k3, p5, k10, p2(4:6).
Row 7: P2(4:6), C10B, p5, k3, p3, k6, p3, k3, p5, C10F, p2(4:6).
Row 9: P2(4:6), k10, p5, k3, p3, C6B, p3, k3, p5, k10, p2(4:6).
Row 11: P2(4:6), k10, p5, k3, C6BP, C6FP, k3, p5, k10, p2(4:6).
Row 12: Knit purl sts and purl knit sts of previous row as they appear, knit bobble sts.

Sleeve
Using US size 3 needles, cast on 56(60:64) sts.
Row 1: [K2, p2] to end of row.
Rep row 1, 7 times more.
Change to US size 6 needles.

101

Shape raglan sleeve top

Row 9: Bind off 2 sts (1 st on right-hand needle), p1(3:5), C10B, p5, C6B, p6, C6F, p5, C10F, p4(6:8). *54(58:62) sts*

Row 10: Bind off 2 sts and patt as for WS row to end of row. *52(56:60) sts*

Keeping patt correct as set, dec 1 st at each end of every alt row for 30 rows. *22(26:30) sts*

Leave sts on a stitch holder.

FINISHING

Weave in loose ends.

Steam the pieces following directions on the yarn label.

Neckband

RS facing, slip sleeve, front, sleeve, back onto a US size 3 needle.

Size 3–4 only

Row 1 (RS): [K2, p2] 10 times, k2 across back, [p2tog twice, k2tog twice] twice, [p2tog] twice, k2 across sleeve, [p2, k2] 9 times, p2 across front, [k2tog twice, p2tog twice] twice, [k2tog] twice, p2 across sleeve. *104 sts*

Size 5–6 only

Row 1 (RS): [K2, p2] 12 times, k2 across back, [p2 tog twice, k2tog twice] 3 times, p2 across sleeve, [k2tog] twice, [p2tog] twice, [k2, p2] 7 times , k2, [p2tog] twice, [k2tog] twice across front, [p2 tog twice, k2tog twice] 3 times, p2 across sleeve. *116 sts*

Size 7–8 only

Row 1 (RS): [K2, p2] 13 times, k2 across back, p1, p2tog, [k2tog twice, p2tog twice] 3 times, k2tog, k1 across sleeve, [p2tog] twice, [k2tog] twice, [p2, k2] 8 times, p2, [k2tog] twice, [p2tog] twice across front, k1, k2tog, [p2tog twice, k2tog twice] 3 times, p2tog, p1 across sleeve. *128 sts*

All sizes

Row 2: [K2, p2] to end of row.

Rep the last row 5 times more.

Bind off.

Sew up the raglans. Sew up the underarm and side seams from end of sleeve to lower edge of body.

Isabel Cable and Little Branch Dress

Emilia Mohair Lace Dress

Please amend as follows: "Here is a simple lace pattern that makes a lovely dress to wear all year. Since working with mohair can be a bit tricky, this pattern is worked with two strands of yarn together, to make things easier. The light dress is perfect to layer over a long jersey top or a T-shirt and leggings.

MEASUREMENTS

Size	3–4 yrs	5–6 yrs	7–8 yrs
To fit chest	23 in	24 in	25¼ in
Finished chest measurement	24¾ in	26½ in	30 in
Finished length from armhole to hem	15¼ in	16½ in	18½ in

YARN

4 x ¾ oz balls of Rowan Kidsilk Haze in Majestic 589 used DOUBLE throughout

MATERIALS

Pair of US size 6 knitting needles
Cable needle
Stitch holder
Tapestry needle

GAUGE

17 sts and 22 rows to 4 in over patt using US size 6 needles and two strands of yarn held together

ABBREVIATIONS

See page 140

LACE PATTERN

(7 sts to 8 sts to 9 sts, plus 2 edge sts—note that the number of sts alternates)

Row 1 (RS): K1, [k6, p1, yo] to last st, k1.

Row 2 and all even-numbered rows: Knit the knit sts and purl the purl sts as they appear, and purl yarnovers.

Row 3: K1, [k6, p2, yo] to last st, k1.

Row 5: K1, [slip next 3 sts onto cable needle and hold at back of work, k3tog from left-hand needle, k3 from cable needle, p3] to last st, k1.

Row 7: K1, [yo, p1, k6] to last st, k1.

Row 9: K1, [yo, p2, k6] to last st, k1.

Row 11: K1, [p3, slip next 3 sts onto cable needle and hold in front of work, k3, k3togtbl from cable needle] to last st, k1.

Row 12: Work sts in patt.

Rep these 12 rows.

BACK

Using 2 strands of yarn, cast on 53(58:65) sts. Knit 8 rows.

Row 9: K1(0:0), then work in patt to last 1(0:0) sts, k1(0:0).

Row 10: P1(0:0), then work in patt to last 1(0:0) sts, p1(0:0).

Keeping patt with edge sts correct as set, cont until work measures 15¼(16½:18½) in from cast on edge, ending with a 6th or 12th patt row.

Shape armholes

Keeping patt correct as set, bind off 4 sts at beg of next 2 rows.

Dec 1 st at each end of next and every alt row for next 4 rows. *41(46:53) sts*

Work in patt for 18 rows.

Shape neck

Patt 10(12:14) sts, k2tog, k1, turn (leave rem sts on a stitch holder). *12(14:16) sts*

Dec 1 st at neck edge on next 2(4:4) rows.
10(10:12) sts

Size 3–4 only

Patt 2 rows.

All sizes

Shape shoulder

Next row: P4(4:6), turn.

Next row: K4(4:6), turn.

Bind off all sts.

RS facing, slip rem sts from the stitch holder onto a needle and re-join yarn.

Next row: Bind off 15(16:19) sts (1 st on right-hand needle), ssk, patt to end of row.

Working patt where possible, shape as folls:

Emilia Mohair Lace Dress

Dec 1 st at neck edge on next 2(4:4) rows.
10(10:12) sts
Patt 3(1:1) rows.
Next row: K4(4:6), turn.
Next row: P4(4:6), turn.
Bind off all sts.

FRONT

Using 2 strands of yarn, cast on 53(58:65) sts.
Knit 8 rows.
Row 9: K1(0:0), work in patt to last 1(0:0) sts,
k1(0:0).
Row 10: P1(0:0), work in patt to last 1(0:0) sts,
p1(0:0).
Keeping patt with edge sts correct as set, cont
until work measures 15¼(16½:18½) in from cast
on edge, ending with a 6th or 12th patt row.
Shape armholes
Keeping patt correct as set, bind off 4 sts at beg of
next 2 rows.
Dec 1 st at each end of next and every alt row for
next 4 rows. *41(46:53) sts*
Work in patt for 6(12:12) rows.
Shape neck
Next row: Patt 14(16:18), k2tog, k1, turn (leave
rem sts on a stitch holder). *16(18:20) sts*
Work each side of neck separately, and where it is
not possible to work a whole patt rep, work st st.

Keeping patt correct as set, dec 1 st at neck edge on next 6(8:8) rows. *10(10:12) sts*
Patt 10(2:2) rows.

Shape shoulder

Next row: WS facing, p4(4:6), turn.
Next row: K4(4:6), turn.
Bind off all sts.
RS facing, slip rem sts from the stitch holder onto a needle and re-join yarn.
Bind off 7(8:11) sts (1 st on right-hand needle), ssk, patt to end of row. *16(18:20) sts*
Keeping patt correct as set, dec 1 st at neck edge on next 6(8:8) rows. *10(10:12) sts*
Patt 11(3:3) rows.

Shape shoulder

Next row: K4(4:6), turn.
Next row: P4(4:6), turn.
Bind off all sts.

Sleeve (make two)

Using 2 strands of yarn, cast on 40 sts.
Rows 1–2: Knit.
Row 3: K14, inc into each of next 12 sts, k14. *52 sts*
Row 4: Knit.
Dec 1 st at each end of every row for 19 rows.
14 sts
Bind off all sts.

Finishing

Weave in loose ends.
Steam the pieces following directions on the yarn label.
Sew up shoulder seams. Then fold each sleeve RS together vertically down the middle and stitch the top "corner" (a line of about ¾ in), then turn RS out. Making sure that the middle of the sleeve aligns with the shoulder seam, sew the top edge of the sleeve into the armhole, but do not sew any of the sleeve to bound off sts underarm. Sew up the side seams.
If you wish, you can make a double crochet loop edge around the neck.

Emilia Mohair Lace Dress

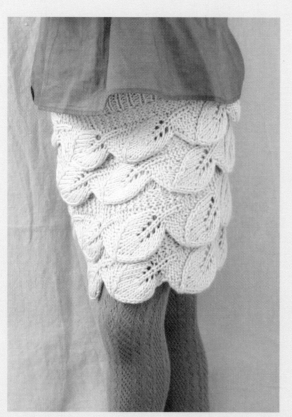

Skirts and Wraps

Flora Layered Leaf Skirt

Leafy layers on a summer skirt. If you prefer ruffles, you can knit the layers longer and ruffle them up when joining them.

MEASUREMENTS

Size	3–4 yrs	5–6 yrs	7–8 yrs
To fit hip	24½ in	25¼ in	27 in
Finished hip measurement	24½ in	25¼ in	27 in

YARN

3(4:4) x 1¾ oz balls of Louisa Harding Albero in Rice 02

MATERIALS

Pair each of US size 6 and US size 3 knitting needles
Spare US size 6 knitting needle
Tapestry needle
1in elastic to fit waist

GAUGE

18 sts and 20 rows to 4 in over st st using US size 6 needles

ABBREVIATIONS

See page 140

Leaf layer

(Note that number of sts alternates)
**Using US size 6 needles, cast on 8 sts.
Row 1: Knit.
Row 2: Purl.
Row 3 (RS): K5, yo, k1, yo, k2.
Row 4: P6, inc, k3.
Row 5: K4, p1, k2, yo, k1, yo, k3.
Row 6: P8, inc, k4.
Row 7: K4, p2, k3, yo, k1, yo, k4.
Row 8: P10, inc, k5.
Row 9: K4, p3, k4, yo, k1, yo, k5.
Row 10: P12, inc, k6. *20 sts*
Row 11: K4, p4, ssk, k7, k2tog, k1.
Row 12: P10, inc, k7.
Row 13: K4, p5, ssk, k5, k2tog, k1.
Row 14: P8, inc, k2, p1, k5.
Row 15: K4, p1, k1, p4, ssk, k3, k2tog, k1.
Row 16: P6, inc, k3, p1, k5.
Row 17: K4, p1, k1, p5, ssk, k1, k2tog, k1.
Row 18: P4, inc, k4, p1, k5.
Row 19: K4, p1, k1, p6, sk2po, k1.
Row 20: P2tog, using st on needle from p2tog
bind off 5 sts, p4 including st used to bind off, k4.
Rep rows 3–20 until you have 8(9:9) leaves
in total.
Bind off.**
Rep from ** to ** 3 times more.

Joining layers

Using US size 6 needles and with RS of bottom
layer facing, pick up 110(124:124) sts evenly
along the garter st edge.
Next row: P to end, dec 8 sts evenly on size 5–6
only. *110(116:124) sts*
Starting with a k row, work 12 rows st st. Leave
sts on needle.
***Using US size 6 needles and with RS of
second layer facing, pick up 110(124:124) sts
evenly along the edge.
Next row: P to end, dec 8 sts evenly on size 5–6
only. *110(116:124) sts*
RS facing, hold second layer in front of bottom
layer, with RS of bottom layer against WS of
second layer, aligning needles. Using spare
US size 6 needle, knit 1 st from each layer
together across the row.***
Starting with a p row, work 13 rows st st.
Work from *** to *** to join third layer to
second layer.
Starting with a p row, work 13 rows st st.
Work from *** to *** to join top layer to
third layer.
Change to US size 3 needles.
Next row: P to end, dec 16 sts evenly. *94(100:108) sts*
Next row: [K1, p1] to end of row.
Rep last row 21 times more.
Bind off.

Flora Layered Leaf Skirt

FINISHING

Weave in loose ends.

Press the pieces following directions on the
yarn label.

Sew up the side seam without sewing the leaves
together. Sew the ends of the elastic together,
checking that it fits comfortably around the
child's waist. Fold the waist rib in half and slip the
circle of elastic into the fold. Slip stitch the bound
off edge to the inside.

Mia Raspberry Mini Skirt

Add a colorful mini skirt to a neutral pair of leggings. Although the raspberry stitch does take a bit of time to knit, it is a lovely pattern and choosing your own ribbon makes the finished piece unique. Can also be worn as a cozy wrap.

MEASUREMENTS

Size	3–4 yrs	5–6 yrs	7–8 yrs
To fit hip	24 in	25 in	26½ in
Finished hip measurement	24¾ in	26¼ in	27¾ in

YARN

3 x 1¾ oz balls of Rowan Pure Wool DK in Geranium 047

MATERIALS

Pair each of US size 3 and US size 6 knitting needles
2 stitch holders
Tapestry needle
Approx 1 yd of 1 in ribbon for the tie
Safety pin or bodkin

GAUGE

30 sts and 24 rows to 4 in over patt using US size 6 needles

ABBREVIATIONS

See page 140

RASPBERRY STITCH PATTERN

(Worked over multiple of 6 sts + 2 edge sts)
Row 1 (RS): Purl.
Row 2: K1, [(k1, p1, k1, p1, k1) all into next st, p5tog] to last st, k1.
Row 3: Purl.
Row 4: K1, [p5tog, (k1, p1, k1, p1, k1) all into next st] to last st, k1.
Rep these 4 rows.

KNITTED IN ONE PIECE

Using US size 3 needles, cast on 188(200:212) sts.
Row 1 (RS): Purl.
Change to US size 6 needles.
Starting with patt row 2, cont in patt until work measures 7½(8:8¼) in from cast on edge, ending with a WS row.
Next row: P1, [k1, p2tog] to last st, k1.
126(134:142) sts
Next row: [P1, k1] to end of row.
Next row: Work p1, k1 rib for 63(67:71) sts, turn (leave rem sts on a stitch holder).

Cont in rib as set for 6 more rows.
Cut yarn and leave these sts on a stitch holder.
Slip 63(67:71) sts from first stitch holder onto a needle.
Next row: [K1, p1] to last st, k1.
Cont in rib as set for 6 more rows.
Slip rem sts from stitch holder onto a needle.
Cont in k1, p1 rib across all 126(134:142) sts until rib measures 2½ in in total.
Bind off.

FINISHING

Weave in loose ends.
Steam the pieces following directions on the yarn label.
Sew up the seam.
Fold the rib in half to the back and slip stitch bound off edge in place to make a channel for the ribbon.
Using a safety pin or a bodkin, slip the ribbon through the channel and tie a bow in the front.

Mia Raspberry Mini Skirt

Skye Big Wool Wrap or Mini Skirt

This is a two-in-one piece as it can work both as a wrap and as a mini skirt. The latter is lovely layered over a pair of leggings.

MEASUREMENTS

Size	3–4 yrs	5–6 yrs	7–8 yrs
To fit hip	24¼ in	25¼ in	27 in
Finished hip measurement	25 in	25¾ in	27½ in

YARN

3(4:4) x 1¾ oz balls of Garnstudio Drops Eskimo in Medium Grey 46

MATERIALS

Pair each of US size 10½ and US size 11 knitting needles
Cable needle
Tapestry needle
Elastic (optional)

GAUGE

9 sts and 19 rows to 4 in over seed stitch using US size 11 needles

C4B—slip next 2 sts onto cable needle and hold at back of work, knit next 2 sts from left-hand needle, then knit 2 sts from cable needle.

C4F—slip next 2 sts onto cable needle and hold in front of work, knit next 2 sts from left-hand needle, then knit 2 sts from cable needle.

C14B—slip next 7 sts onto cable needle and hold at back of work, knit next 7 sts from left-hand needle, turn, purl the same 7 sts, turn, knit the same 7 sts again, then knit the 7 sts from the cable needle, turn, purl the same 7 sts, turn, then knit the same 7 sts again.

See also page 140

KNITTED IN ONE PIECE

Using US size 10½ needles, cast on 78(82:86) sts.
Rows 1–5: [K1, p1] to end of row.
Change to US size 11 needles.
Row 6: [P1, k1] 7(8:9) times, p1, k4, p1, k14, p1, k4, [k1, p1] 7(8:9) times, k1, k4, p1, k14, p1, k4.
Row 7: P4, k1, p14, k1, p4, [k1, p1] 7(8:9) times, k1, p4, k1, p14, k1, p4, [p1, k1] 7(8:9) times, p1.
Row 8: [P1, k1] 7(8:9) times, p1, C4B, p1, C14B, p1, C4F, [k1, p1] 7(8:9) times, k1, C4B, p1, C14B, p1, C4F.

Row 9: P4, k1, p14, k1, p4, [k1, p1] 7(8:9) times, k1, p4, k1, p14, k1, p4, [p1, k1] 7(8:9) times, p1.
Row 10: As row 6.
Row 11: As row 7.
Row 12: [P1, k1] 7(8:9) times, p1, C4B, p1, k14, p1, C4F, [k1, p1] 7(8:9) times, k1, C4B, p1, k14, p1, C4F.
Row 13: P4, k1, p14, k1, p4, [k1, p1] 7(8:9) times, k1, p4, k1, p14, k1, p4, [p1, k1] 7(8:9) times, p1.
Rep rows 6–13 twice more, then rep rows 6–11 once more.
Change to US size 10½ needles.
Rows 36–39: [K1, p1] to end of row.
Bind off.

FINISHING

Weave in loose ends.
Steam the pieces following directions on the yarn label.
Sew up the seam using mattress stitch.
If the piece is only going to be worn as a skirt, you may want to sew a length of elastic to the inside of the rib for a snugger fit around the waist.

Skye Big Wool Wrap or Mini Skirt

Charming Accessories

Laura Frost Flower
Hat and Poncho

I fell for this stitch pattern the minute I saw it, but it was a while before I finally found the instructions so I could try it out. Both hat and poncho are one-size pieces, but if you think they will be too large for your child, try swatching the pattern in a slightly thinner yarn.

MEASUREMENTS

Size	5–8 yrs
To fit chest	24–25¼ in
Finished chest measurement	35½ in at the widest point
To fit head	20½–21¼ in
Finished head measurement	18⅞ in

YARN

2 x 3½ oz balls of Rowan Cocoon in Clay 825

MATERIALS

Pair each of US size 8 and US size 10 knitting needles
Tapestry needle

GAUGE

14 sts and 18 rows to 4 in over st st using US size 10 needles

ABBREVIATIONS

See page 140

PONCHO

Using US size 8 needles, cast on 136 sts.
Row 1: [K1, p1] to end of row.
Rep row 1, 5 times more.
Change to US size 10 needles.
Row 7: [K3, k2tog, k4, yo, p2, (k2, yo, ssk)
3 times, p2, yo, k4, ssk, k3] 4 times.
Row 8: [P2, p2togtbl, p4, yo, p1, k2, (p2, yo,
p2tog) 3 times, k2, p1, yo, p4, p2tog, p2] 4 times.
Row 9: [K1, k2tog, k4, yo, k2, p2, (k2, yo, ssk)
3 times, p2, k2, yo, k4, ssk, k1] 4 times.
Row 10: [P2togtbl, p4, yo, p3, k2, (p2, yo, p2tog)
3 times, k2, p3, yo, p4, p2tog] 4 times.
Rep rows 7–10, 4 times more.
Row 27: [K10, ssk, k2, ssk, k2, k2tog, k2, k2tog,
k10] 4 times. *120 sts*
Row 28 and all WS rows: Purl.
Row 29: [Ssk, k18, ssk, k16, k2tog, k18, k2tog]
twice. *112 sts*
Row 31: [Ssk, k17, ssk, k14, k2tog, k17, k2tog]
twice. *104 sts*
Row 33: [Ssk, k16, ssk, k12, k2tog, k16, k2tog]
twice. *96 sts*
Row 35: [Ssk, k15, ssk, k10, k2tog, k15, k2tog]
twice. *88 sts*
Row 37: [Ssk, k14, ssk, k8, k2tog, k14, k2tog]
twice. *80 sts*
Change to US size 8 needles.
Row 39: [K1, p1] to end of row.

Rep row 39, 4 times more.
Bind off.

FINISHING

Weave in loose ends.
Steam the pieces following directions on the
yarn label.
Sew up the side seam.

HAT

Using US size 8 needles, cast on 70 sts.
Row 1: [K1, p1] to end of row.
Rep row 1 twice more.
Change to US size 10 needles.
Row 4: K1, [k3, k2tog, k4, yo, p2, (k2, yo, ssk)
3 times, p2, yo, k4, ssk, k3] twice, k1.
Row 5: K1, [p2, p2togtbl, p4, yo, p1, k2,
(p2, yo, p2tog) 3 times, k2, p1, yo, p4, p2tog, p2]
twice, k1.
Row 6: K1, [k1, k2tog, k4, yo, k2, p2, (k2, yo, ssk)
3 times, p2, k2, yo, k4, ssk, k1] twice, k1.
Row 7: K1, [p2togtbl, p4, yo, p3, k2, (p2, yo,
p2tog) 3 times, k2, p3, yo, p4, p2tog] twice, k1.
Rep rows 4–7 twice more.
Row 16: Knit.
Row 17: Purl.

Laura Frost Flower Hat and Poncho

Rep rows 16–17 twice more.
Row 22: [K5, k2tog] to end of row. *60 sts*
Row 23 and all WS rows: Purl.
Row 24: [K4, k2tog] to end of row. *50 sts*
Row 26: [K3, k2tog] to end of row. *40 sts*
Row 28: [K2, k2tog] to end of row. *30 sts*
Row 30: [K1, k2tog] to end of row. *20 sts*
Row 32: [K2tog] to end of row. *10 sts*
Work 4 rows st st.
Bind off, knitting 2 sts together each time before passing over.

FINISHING

Weave in loose ends.
Steam the pieces following directions on the yarn label.
Sew up the side seam.

Naya Garter Stitch Scarf and Hat with Eyelets

A colorful way of keeping warm, these are super-stylish accessories to wear with a simple shirt or dress.

MEASUREMENTS

Size	3–4 yrs	5–6 yrs	7–8 yrs
Scarf length	45 in	45 in	45 in
Hat to fit head	19¼ in	20½ in	21¼ in
Finished head measurement	16 in	17½ in	19¼ in

YARN

2 x 1¾ oz balls of Rowan by Amy Butler Belle Organic Aran in Slate 210 (A)
1 x 1¾ oz ball of Rowan by Amy Butler Belle Organic Aran in Poppy 206 (B)

MATERIALS

Pair each of US size 6 and US size 7 knitting needles
Pair of US size 6 double-pointed needles
Tapestry needle

GAUGE

18 sts and 32 rows to 4 in over garter stitch using US size 7 needles

yo2—yarn over needle twice.
G4—gather 4 sts: slip 4 sts purlwise (yarn at back of work) onto right-hand needle, dropping the yarnovers off needle and stretching the sts, pass the 4 sts back onto the left-hand needle, then work (purl, knit, purl, knit) into all 4 sts together, slip the sts off the left-hand needle.
See also page 140

SCARF

Using US size 6 needles and A, cast on 24 sts.
Rows 1–5: Knit.
Change to US size 7 needles.
Row 6: [K1, yo2] to last st, k1.
Row 7: [G4] to end of row.
Rows 8–11: Knit.
Row 12: [K1, yo2] to last st, k1.
Row 13: [G4] to end of row.
Rep rows 8–13 once more.
Rows 20–22: Knit.
Change to US size 6 needles and B.
Row 23: [K2tog] to end of row. *12 sts*
Rows 24–34: Knit.
Change to US size 7 needles and A.
Row 35: Knit. *12 sts*
Row 36: Inc into every st. *24 sts*

Naya Garter Stitch Scarf and Hat with Eyelets

Rows 37–39: Knit.
Rep rows 6–39, 6 times more, or as preferred for a shorter or longer scarf.
Rep rows 6–11, 3 times more.
Bind off all sts.

HAT

Using US size 6 needles and A, cast on 72(80:88) sts.
Rows 1–9: Knit.
Change to US size 7 needles.
Row 10: [K1, yo2] to last st, k1.
Row 11: [G4] to end of row.
Rows 12–17: Knit.
Row 18: [K1, yo2] to last st, k1.
Row 19: [G4] to end of row.
Change to US size 6 needles.
Knit 18(22:26) rows.
Row 38(42:46): [K6, k2tog] to end of row. *63(70:77) sts*
Row 39(43:47): Knit.
Row 40(44:48): [K5, k2tog] to end of row. *54(60:66) sts*
Row 41(45:49): Knit.
Row 42(46:50): [K4, k2tog] to end of row. *45(50:55) sts*
Row 43(47:51): Knit.
Row 44(48:52): [K3, k2tog] to end of row. *36(40:44) sts*

Row 45(49:53): Knit.
Row 46(50:54): [K2, k2tog] to end of row. *27(30:33) sts*
Row 47(51:55): Knit.
Row 48(52:56): [K1, k2tog] to end of row. *18(20:22) sts*
Row 49(53:57): Knit.
Row 50(54:58): [K2tog] to end of row. *9(10:11) sts*
Row 51(55:59): Knit.
Change to US size 6 double-pointed needles and B.
Row 52(56:60): [K2tog] 1(2:3) times, k3(2:1), [k2tog] twice. *6 sts*
Work i-cord as folls:
Slide sts just knitted to other end of needle. Take yarn across back of work. Knit sts again, pulling yarn tight to knit first st. Cont until i-cord measures 5 in.
Bind off.

FINISHING

Weave in loose ends.
Steam the pieces following directions on the yarn label.
Sew up hat seam and tie i-cord in a knot.

Olivia Mohair Scarf with Bobbles

This very pretty scarf works all year round and, most unusually, looks good on both sides.

MEASUREMENTS

Size   one size
Finished measurements   35½ x 18¼ in

YARN

3 x ¾ oz balls of Rowan Kidsilk Haze in Pearl 590 used DOUBLE throughout

MATERIALS

Pair of US size 6 knitting needles
Tapestry needle

GAUGE

15 sts and 22 rows to 4 in over patt using US size 6 needles and two strands of yarn held together

Note: This scarf can easily be made up as a smaller size or a bigger size. Cast on a number of sts divisible by 22 and work patt as described below. Work first half as described in patt A, then work second half in patt B. Just remember you might need extra yarn.

ABBREVIATIONS

MB—make bobble: (k1, p1, k1, p1) all into next st, turn, p4, turn, k4, pass 2nd, 3rd and 4th sts over last st on right-hand needle.
See also page 140

PATTERN A

(Worked over multiple of 11 sts and 16 rows)
Row 1: K2tog, yo, k1, yo, k6, ssk.
Row 2 and every alt row: Purl.
Row 3: K2tog, k1, yo, k1, yo, k5, ssk.
Row 5: K2tog, k2, yo, k1, yo, k4, ssk.
Row 7: K2tog, k2, MB, yo, k1, yo, k3, ssk.
Row 9: K2tog, k3, MB, yo, k1, yo, k2, ssk.
Row 11: K2tog, k4, MB, yo, k1, yo, k1, ssk.
Row 13: K2tog, k5, MB, yo, k1, yo, ssk.
Row 15: K2tog, yo, k1, yo, k5, MB, ssk.
Row 16: Purl.

PATTERN B

(Worked over multiple of 11 sts and 16 rows)
Row 1: K2tog, k6, yo, k1, yo, ssk.
Row 2 and every alt row: Purl.
Row 3: K2tog, k5, yo, k1, yo, k1, ssk.
Row 5: K2tog, k4, yo, k1, yo, k2, ssk.
Row 7: K2tog, k3, yo, k1, yo, MB, k2, ssk.
Row 9: K2tog, k2, yo, k1, yo, MB, k3, ssk.
Row 11: K2tog, k1, yo, k1, yo, MB, k4, ssk.
Row 13: K2tog, yo, k1, yo, MB, k5, ssk.
Row 15: K2tog, MB, k5, yo, k1, yo, ssk.
Row 16: Purl.

SCARF

Using 2 strands of yarn, cast on 133 sts.
Row 1 (WS): Purl.
Row 2: MB, [k2, MB] to end of row.
Row 3: Purl, dec 1 st in center of row, **at the same time** on approx every 3rd st pick up loop from the bottom row and work it together with the st on the needle. This will give a more "bobbly" edge. Alternatively, you can just purl the row. *132 sts*
Row 4: Making a bobble from the first k2tog, work row 1 of patt A for 6 reps, then work row 1 of patt B for 6 reps, making a bobble from the last ssk.
Row 5 and every alt row: Purl.
Row 6: K3tog, yo, k1, yo, k5, ssk, then work row 3 of patt A for 5 reps, then work row 3 of patt B for 5 reps, then k2tog, k5, yo, k1, yo, k3tog. Keeping patt A and patt B correct, cont as folls:
Row 8: K3tog and make bobble from this st, yo, k1, yo, k4, ssk, then work patt A for 5 reps, then work patt B for 5 reps, then k2tog, k4, yo, k1, yo, k3tog and make bobble from this st.

Olivia Mohair Scarf with Bobbles

Row 10: K3tog, yo, k1, yo, k3, ssk, then work patt A for 5 reps, then work patt B for 5 reps, then k2tog, k3, yo, k1, yo, k3tog.

Row 12: K3tog and make bobble from this st, yo, k1, yo, k2, ssk, then work patt A for 5 reps, then work patt B for 5 reps, then k2tog, k2, yo, k1, yo, k3tog and make bobble from this st.

Row 14: K3tog, yo, k1, yo, k1, ssk, then work patt A for 5 reps, then work patt B for 5 reps, then k2tog, k1, yo, k1, yo, k3tog.

Row 16: K3tog and make bobble from this st, yo, k1, yo, ssk, then work patt A for 5 reps, then work patt B for 5 reps, then k2tog, yo, k1, yo, k3tog and make bobble from this st.

Row 18: K3tog, ssk, then work patt A for 5 reps, then work patt B for 5 reps, then k2tog, k3tog.

Row 20: K4tog and make bobble from this st, yo, k1, yo, k6, ssk, then work row 1 of patt A for 4 reps, then work row 1 of patt B for 4 reps, then k2tog, k6, yo, k1, yo, k4tog and make bobble from this st.

Keeping patt correct as set, continue dec 1 st at each end of foll alt rows (by knitting 3 sts together on right side) and making a bobble at each end on every 4th row. On row 1 of every foll patt rep, dec by knitting 4 sts together at each side.

When you have 4 sts left, knit these together and make a bobble.

FINISHING

Weave in loose ends.
Steam the pieces following directions on the yarn label.

Olivia Mohair Scarf with Bobbles

Abbreviations

alt	alternate; alternatively
approx	approximately
beg	begin(s)(ning)
C4B	cable four stitches (or number stated) back
C4F	cable four stitches (or number stated) front
cont	continue
dec	decrease(s)(ing)
DK	double knit
foll(s)	follow(s)(ing)
G4	gather four stitches
in	inch(es)
inc	increase(s)(ing)
k	knit
k2tog	knit two stitches (or number stated) together
k2togtbl	knit two stitches (or number stated) together through the back loops
MB	make bobble
MK	make knot
ML	make loop
oz	ounce(s)
p	purl
p2tog	purl two stitches (or number stated) together

p2togtbl	purl two stitches (or number stated) together through the back loops
patt(s)	pattern(s)
rem	remain(ing)
rep(s)	repeat(s)
RS	right side
skpo	slip one stitch, knit one stitch, pass slipped stitch over
sk2po	slip one stitch, knit two stitches together, pass slipped stitch over
ssk	slip one stitch, slip one stitch, knit slipped stitches together through the back loops
st st	stockinette stitch
st(s)	stitch(es)
tbl	through back of loop
tog	together
WS	wrong side
yo	yarn over needle
yo2	yarn over needle twice
yr(s)	year(s)
*	repeat instruction after/between * as many times as stated
[ ]	repeat instructions between [ ] as many times as stated

Choosing Yarn

If you are buying the yarn recommended in the pattern you have chosen to knit, then you just have to choose the color you want. However, if you are substituting another yarn for a recommended pattern yarn, then there are some rules to follow.

Firstly, unless you are practiced at altering patterns, choose a substitute yarn that is the same weight as the pattern yarn—trying to knit a worsted-weight pattern with a fingering-weight yarn will create huge problems. Even if you have chosen a substitute yarn that is the recommended weight, be aware that yarns of the same weight do not always knit up to the same gauge, so you must work a gauge swatch. The yarn label of the substitute yarn will provide an average gauge, and as long as this doesn't differ by more than one stitch from that of the pattern yarn, you should be able to achieve the right gauge by changing needle size. More than one stitch difference could cause problems.

Then you have to work out how much of the substitute yarn you need. You cannot simply buy the amount of yarn stated in the pattern because, even though the balls may weigh the same as those of the pattern yarn, they will not necessarily contain the same number of yards. To work out how much substitute yarn you need, try this formula: Multiply the number of yards per ball/skein by the number of balls/skeins specified in the pattern. This will give you the number of yards needed.

Divide the total number of yards needed by the number of yards in a single ball/skein of the substitute yarn. This will give you the number of balls/skeins needed.

Number of yards of yarn in one ball of pattern yarn, multiplied by the number of balls needed, to give you the total number of yards of yarn needed.

Total number of yards needed, divided by the number of yards of yarn in one ball of the substitute yarn, to give you the number of balls of substitute yarn you need to buy.

For example

125 yards per ball of the pattern yarn, and
15 balls are needed.
125 x 15 = 1875 yards in total of yarn needed.

95 yards per ball of the substitute yarn.
1875 ÷ by 95 = 19.73.
Therefore you will need to buy 20 balls of the substitute yarn.

If you have a good local yarn store then the staff should also be able to help you in making a suitable yarn choice.

If you are using a substitute yarn, it is always worth knitting first the back and then one sleeve. This is approximately halfway through a sweater and you will be able to see whether you are going to have enough yarn to finish the project.

Yarn Information

Debbie Bliss Eco Aran: 82 yd/1¾ oz ball; 100% organic cotton.

Garnstudio Drops Alpaca: 182 yd/1¾ oz ball; 100% pure alpaca.

Garnstudio Drops Eskimo: 54 yd/1¾ oz ball; 100% pure new wool.

Louisa Harding Albero: 109 yd/1¾ oz ball; 50% cotton, 50% lenpur viscose.

Louisa Harding Millais: 65 yd/1¾ oz ball; 50% wool, 50% acrylic.

Mirasol Miski: 82 yd/1¾ oz skein; 100% baby llama.

Mirasol Sulka: 54 yd/1¾ oz skein; 60% merino wool, 20% alpaca, 20% silk.

Rowan Alpaca Cotton: 147 yd/1¾ oz ball; 72% alpaca, 28% cotton.

Rowan by Amy Butler Belle Organic Aran: 98 yd/1¾ oz ball; 50% organic wool, 50% organic cotton.

Rowan by Amy Butler Belle Organic DK: 131 yd/1¾ oz ball; 50% organic wool, 50% organic cotton.

Rowan Cashsoft DK: 125 yd/1¾ oz ball; 57% extra fine merino, 33% acrylic microfibre, 10% cashmere.

Rowan Cocoon: 125 yd/3½ oz ball; 80% merino wool, 20% kid mohair.

Rowan Drift: 87 yd/3½ oz ball; 100% merino wool.

Rowan Kidsilk Haze: 229 yd/¾ oz ball; 70% super kid mohair, 30% silk.

Rowan Lima: 109 yd/1¾ oz ball; 84% baby alpaca, 8% merino wool, 8% nylon.

Rowan Pure Wool DK: 136 yd/1¾ oz ball; 100% superwash wool.

UK Alpaca DK: 144 yd/1¾ oz ball; 70% fine grade UK alpaca, 30% British Blueface Leicester wool.

Suppliers

Debbie Bliss
www.knittingfever.com

Garnstudio Drops Design
www.garnstudio.com

Louisa Harding
www.knittingfever.com

Mirasol
www.mirasolperu.com

Rowan
www.knitrowan.com

UK Alpaca
www.ukalpaca.com

Author Acknowledgments

There are quite a few people without whose help and support I could never have done this book.

Amy Christian for guiding me through the process of making the book and for trusting that I could do it, and Laura Russell for helping me with the post editing of photos and for the lovely layouts.

Kate Haxell for her support and meticulous editing and Marilyn Wilson for her thorough pattern checking, without which this book would be unreadable.

Kate Buller and David MacLeod from Rowan, Dionne Taylor from Designer Yarns, and Chas Brooke from UK Alpaca for providing me with a wheelbarrow full of luxurious yarns.

My wonderful models, Olivia, Lirio, and Silje, and their families for their patience and helpfulness.

My loving partner, Antonio, for his never-yielding support and comfort.

My whole family, always there, always helping, always supporting.

My friends who have always encouraged me.

Standard Yarn Weights

Yarn Weight Symbol and Category Name	Super Fine **1**	Fine **2**	Light **3**	Medium **4**	Bulky **5**	Super Bulky **6**
Types of yarn in category	Sock, fingering, baby	Sport, baby	DK, light worsted	Worsted, afghan, Aran	Chunky, craft, rug	Bulky, roving
Knit gauge range in St st in 4 in.	27–32 sts	23–26 sts	21–24 sts	16–20 sts	12–15 sts	6–11 sts
Recommended metric needle size	2.25–3.25 mm	3.25–3.75 mm	3.75–4.5 mm	4.5–5.5 mm	5.5–8 mm	8 mm and larger
Recommended U.S. needle size	1–3	3–5	5–7	7–9	9–11	11 and larger
Crochet gauge range in sc in 4 in.	21–31 sts	16–20 sts	12–17 sts	11–14 sts	8–11 sts	5–9 sts
Recommended metric hook size	2.25–3.5 mm	3.5–4.5 mm	4.5–5.5 mm	5.5–6.5 mm	6.5–9 mm	9 mm and larger
Recommended U.S. hook size	B/1–E/4	E/4–7	7–I/9	I/9–K/10.5	K/10.5–M/13	M/13 and larger

Categories of yarn, gauge ranges, and recommended knitting needle sizes from the Craft Yarn Council of America.

GUIDELINES ONLY: The information in this table reflects the most commonly used gauges and needle or hook sizes for the specific yarn categories. The generic yarn-weight names in the yarn categories include those most commonly used in the US and UK. Ultra-fine lace-weight yarns are difficult to put in gauge ranges; always follow the gauge given in your pattern for these yarns.

Knitting Needle Sizes

MILLIMETER RANGE	U.S. SIZE RANGE	MILLIMETER RANGE	U.S. SIZE RANGE
2.25mm	1	6mm	10
2.75mm	2	6.5mm	10½
3.25mm	3	8mm	11
3.5mm	4	9mm	13
3.75mm	5	10mm	15
4mm	6	12.75mm	17
4.5mm	7	15mm	19
5mm	8	19mm	35
5.5mm	9	25mm	50

To place an order or to request a catalog, contact
The Taunton Press, Inc.
63 South Main Street, P.O. Box 5506, Newtown, CT 06470-5506
Tel (800) 888-8286

www. taunton.com